Editorial Planning and Layout *Tim Healey*
Co-ordinating Editor *Lis Edwards*
Managing Editor *Philippa Stewart*
Production *Rosemary Bishop*
Picture Research *Georgina Barker*

First published 1980
Macdonald Educational Ltd
Holywell House
Worship Street
London EC2A 2EN

©Macdonald Educational Ltd 1980
Adapted and published in
the United States by
Silver Burdett Company,
Morristown, N.J.
1980 Printing

ISBN 0-382-06413-5
Library of Congress
Catalog Card No. 80-52505

TIMESPAN
EXPLORERS

WRITTEN AND DEVISED BY TIM HEALEY

CONTENTS

Introduction

When the mountaineer George Mallory was asked *why* he was so keen to climb Mount Everest he answered, "because it is there". His reply was not just a joke. It hints at an urge to conquer the unknown that seems part of human nature.

Explorers have had many reasons for setting out across the world. Some, like Hernando Cortés, the Spanish conqueror, were fired by the lust for gold. Others were exploring rich trade routes, like Marco Polo. David Livingstone went to Africa as a missionary. René de La Salle explored North America in order to build up an empire. Horace De Saussure was driven by scientific curiosity to launch the world's first true mountaineering expedition.

But most of these explorers also knew the thrill of discovery for its own sake. Captain Cook described "the pleasure which naturally results to a man from being the first discoverer, even was it of nothing more than sands or shoals".

All great explorers faced the challenge of the elements, and it often brought out the best in them. As Captain Scott lay dying of cold and starvation in his tent in Antarctica, he had no regrets about the way he had chosen to live his life. "How much better all this has been than lounging in too much comfort at home," he wrote in his diary.

The wandering urge goes back to the dawn of history. Our ancestors were hunters, forced by hunger to follow their prey into unfamiliar woods, plains and valleys. Some left their homelands and put out to sea in frail craft. Through their wanderings these early peoples gradually populated almost all the world's land masses. Only Antarctica remained uninhabited.

Neither Columbus, nor the Vikings, were the first to discover America. The native Americans were already there. Their ancestors were an Asiatic people who had crossed over into Alaska hundreds of thousands of years earlier, spreading southward throughout the whole continent. So when we speak of people such as Columbus "discovering" new lands, we mean that they have reached places previously unknown to them. Of course, they were not unknown to the people who lived there.

Primitive people may have been the first explorers, but they had no idea of the world's true shape, of the extent of its oceans and continents. Through generations of exploration, these have slowly been revealed. Explorers have charted lands and seas, filling in blank areas to produce the world map we know today.

There are no new lands left to discover on earth. Yet more than two-thirds of the earth's surface is covered by oceans, and we are only just beginning to explore their depths. Beyond our world lies the infinity of space. We have begun to explore other planets. As one age of discovery comes to an end, new ages are dawning.

◀ Footprints on the moon; an American astronaut collects rock samples from the lunar surface.

Around Africa

The Phoenician circumnavigation, c. 600 BC

"As for Africa," wrote Herodotus, "we know that it is washed on all sides by the sea, except where it joins Asia." He was quite right. But *how* did this ancient Greek historian know the shape of the vast continent?

Herodotus wrote that, in about 600 BC, Egypt's pharaoh Necho II was planning to dig a canal between the Red Sea and the River Nile. This would let ships pass through to the Mediterranean Sea. However, he abandoned the project. Instead, he decided to see whether a route to the Mediterranean could be found by sailing round the uncharted coast of Africa.

Necho chose Phoenicians for the voyage, for they were famed throughout the ancient world for their seafaring skill. A small fleet was gathered and ordered to leave Egypt by the Red Sea.

What perils did the Phoenicians meet as they battled their way down the coast? Did they fight skirmishes with native tribesmen? Were they shipwrecked as they rounded the storm-tossed Cape of Good Hope? We do not know. Herodotus left the only account of the voyage, and it is very short.

He wrote that the Phoenician explorers sailed down the coast until autumn, then went ashore and sowed a piece of land with corn. When it was ready to harvest, they set off again with their store of food. After another year, they went ashore again to sow and harvest. Then they sailed on, and in the third year sighted the Straits of Gibraltar (which they called the Pillars of Hercules). We can imagine their relief as they entered the familiar Mediterranean Sea.

The voyage was an astonishing feat, a trip of more than 20,000 kilometres. No European managed to sail around Africa for another 2000 years. How can we be sure that the Phoenicians really succeeded?

Beak for ramming

Herodotus ended his account with an important remark. He said that the Phoenicians declared that, as they sailed around Africa, the sun was to their north. This must have seemed extraordinary to these peoples. Seen from any land known to them, the sun always rose and set to the *south*. In fact, Herodotus doubted whether the Phoenicians were telling the truth on this point: "I for one do not believe them, though others may."

Yet this one observation suggests that the voyage really did take place, for in order to sail round Africa, you have to cross the equator. Beyond this line, the sun *does* appear to your north. Surely, no one could have invented the observation. It must have made a frightening impression on the Phoenicians.

The Phoenicians were great navigators, but they were very secretive. They explored the seas for trade, and did not want others to know of the routes they discovered. Having sailed around Africa, it is unlikely that they repeated the long and dangerous voyage. They had failed to find a suitable trade route to the Mediterranean. But in searching for it they had made one of the world's greatest voyages of discovery.

Square sail

Steering oar

Banks of oarsmen

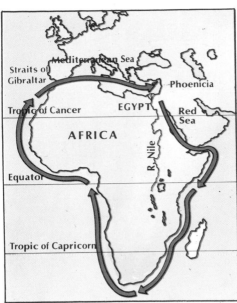

▲ A map of Africa, showing the Phoenician route. The sun never appears overhead north of the Tropic of Cancer, or south of the Tropic of Capricorn. Seen from the Mediterranean, it is always to the south.

◄ We do not know exactly what sort of ships the Phoenicians used on their great voyage. They were probably war galleys, propelled by one or two banks of oarsmen.

Phoenican galleys had a square sail, a steering paddle and an underwater beak at the prow for ramming.

Some historians still doubt whether these ships could have been sailed right round Africa. But by using favourable winds and currents, the Phoenicians could have made the voyage. They only needed to travel about 14 kilometres a day.

◄ Pharaoh Necho (609-594 BC) at first planned to dig a canal between the Red Sea and the Nile.

Such a canal had been built over a thousand years earlier, but it had fallen into disuse.

► The Straits of Gibraltar separate Africa from Europe by a narrow 18-kilometre stretch of sea.

"On their return they declared that in sailing round Libya they had the sun on their right hand. I for one do not believe them, though others may."
HERODOTUS

▲ Herodotus spoke of the Phoenicians having the sun "on their right hand" as they sailed round Libya (Africa). So, since they were sailing westward, the sun was to their north.

Pytheas Sails North
A Greek explorer

▲ Pytheas sailed right around Britain, which he describes as roughly triangular in shape. We do not know whether his "Thule" was Iceland, Norway, the Faroes or the Shetlands. He may have begun his journey by following the overland tin route to Corbilo, rather than sailing through the Straits of Gibraltar.

▼A vase showing the two basic types of Greek ship. On the right is the war galley; on the left, the rounder merchant ship which was propelled entirely by sail power. We do not know which type Pytheas used.

The Ancient Greeks knew the coastline of the Mediterranean, and its seaways were well travelled. But beyond the Straits of Gibraltar lay the stormy Atlantic Ocean, a seemingly endless sea which struck terror into the bravest hearts. Though the Phoenicians had ventured into its cold northern waters, the first recorded voyage was made by a Greek explorer of the 4th century BC. His name was Pytheas and he came from the Greek port of Massilia (Marseilles) in southern France.

The Greeks knew little about northern Europe, except that traders brought tin, amber and lead from its dark forests by long routes over land and sea. Perhaps Pytheas wanted to explore the sea routes for trade. In about 310 BC he set out into the Atlantic, heading north on a great voyage of discovery that was to last six years.

During this time, Pytheas visited Britain, which was known as the Tin Isles. He visited the Cornish tin mines and explored inland. His writings give the first glimpse of the British over 250 years before Caesar arrived.

Pytheas was quite impressed. "Britain," he wrote, "has many kings and rulers who live most of the time in peace with one another. The people are simple in their habits and far removed from the cunning and knavishness of modern man."

But the climate was cold and gloomy. Pytheas noticed that the people had to thresh their grain indoors for fear of rain. There was no wine. Instead, the people drank a kind of mead, called *curmi*, which they made from fermented barley.

Pytheas then sailed to the northern tip of Britain. Six days further on, he reported, was an island called Thule. It was surrounded by a thick, congealed mass, like a sea of jellyfish. We cannot be sure exactly which land he had seen.

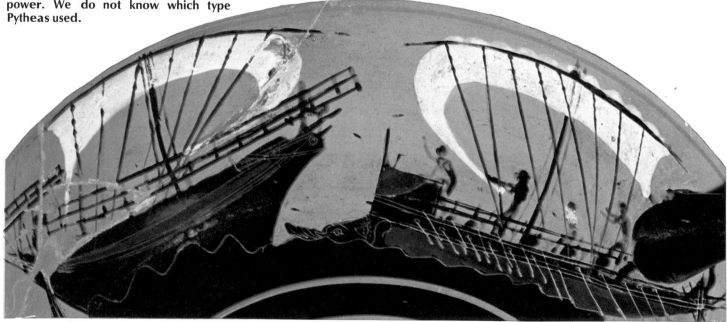

THE TIN TRADE

Pytheas gave a good description of the tin trade. Tin was mined at Land's End in Cornwall *(1)*. It was smelted *(2)* and cast into H-shaped ingots for easy carrying *(3)*; the ingots were 86 centimetres long and weighed 81 kilograms.

The tin was carried in wagons to the island of Ictis (probably St Michael's Mount) and sold to merchants *(4)*. Then it was shipped to Gaul, probably to Corbilo, *(5)*, and carried on pack-horses to Marseilles *(6)*.

The distance from Corbilo to Marseilles is roughly 800 kilometres. Pytheas said that the journey took 30 days, so the pack-horses seem to have covered roughly 23 kilometres a day. Tin was vital to metalworkers, since it was used to make bronze.

Thule may have been the Hebrides, Iceland, or the coast of Norway. The "jellyfish" may have been blocks of ice, known as pancake ice. Beyond Thule, said Pytheas, was the northern limit of the world. It was a place where the sun never slept and the nights sometimes lasted only two hours. This suggests that he may have gone inside the Arctic Circle.

Pytheas noticed that summer days lasted longer the further north he travelled. (By recording their length, you can find out how far north you are.) He discovered that the tides are influenced by the phases of the moon. On his return to Marseilles, he wrote two books about his findings.

Unfortunately, neither has survived. All we know about this intrepid explorer comes from the works of later writers, who often laughed at his reports.

Certainly, Pytheas did make mistakes. He was never very good at judging the distances he had travelled. But he had clearly been to the northern fringe of the known world. Like many explorers since then, he was simply not believed when he came home.

▲ When new ice forms at sea, it often appears as round discs known as "pancake ice". This may have caused Pytheas to speak of a sea of jellyfish.

Father and Son

Erik the Red and Leif Eriksson

> *"They went ashore and looked about them. The weather was fine. There was dew on the grass, and the first thing they did was to get some of it on their hands and put it to their lips. To them it seemed the sweetest thing they had ever tasted."*
>
> *VIKING SAGA*

▲ Leif Eriksson's party setting foot on Vinland, as described in a Viking Saga.

▼ Viking traders and raiders travelled to places as far afield as Alexandria and Baghdad.

Sailing west from Greenland, Leif Eriksson probably passed Baffin Island and Labrador before he reached Vinland. We do not know Vinland's exact location. Archaeologists have found a Viking site in Newfoundland, but Leif's settlement was probably further south.

Erik the Red was a sturdy Viking farmer whose hot temper was always leading him into trouble. He was forced to flee Norway "because of some killings", and sailed to the Viking colony in Iceland. Then, in AD 982, he got involved in another feud. He was outlawed; where could he flee to now?

It was rumoured that somewhere across the grey western sea lay an unknown land. Seizing his chance, Erik gathered a crew and set off.

The explorers sailed for many days until they sighted an ice-bound coast, capped by a bleak and towering glacier. They skirted south round the coast until they found a better spot to land.

Here the Vikings built a few rough cabins and set up a farm. The area was grassy, but barren. Erik called it Greenland to make it sound more attractive than it was. And, three years after arriving, he went back to Iceland and persuaded more settlers to return with him and found a colony.

Erik's Greenland settlement grew steadily. The Vikings believed it was the western edge of the world. Then, in AD 985, a man called Bjarni Herjolfsson arrived from Iceland with startling news. He had been blown off-course and sighted lands still further west.

The settlement buzzed with excitement. Some people criticized Bjarni for failing to explore these lands while he had the chance. And eventually, one brave adventurer decided to set off and find them again. He was Leif Eriksson, the son of Erik the Red.

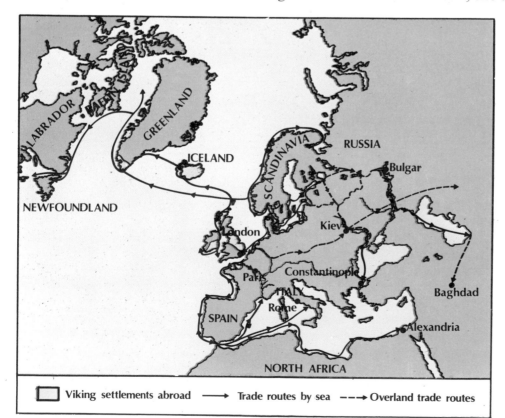

Viking settlements abroad ▢   Trade routes by sea ——➤   Overland trade routes ---➤

▲ An old turf farm in Iceland. The Viking buildings in Greenland probably looked like this.

At L'Anse aux Meadows, in Newfoundland, the Viking settlement included houses, boat sheds, a smith's workshop, a charcoal kiln and cooking pits.

The houses had low turf walls, with turf-covered timber roofs. The site was discovered in 1960, and proves that the Vikings did discover America.

Leif bought Bjarni's ship and assembled a crew of 35 men. Erik agreed to come too, but as they rode to the ship his horse stumbled and threw him. To a Viking, this was a bad omen. Erik changed his mind. "I am not meant to discover more countries than this one," he said. So, in about AD 1000, Leif set off without him.

The Vikings sailed west and reached a flat, rocky land. Further still they sighted a second country. This one was thick with forests. They sailed for two more days and then discovered a third land. The weather was hot, and the weary explorers rushed ashore, plunged their hands into the lush grass and rubbed dew all over their faces. According to a Viking Saga, "it was the sweetest thing they had ever tasted".

The rivers held the biggest salmon they had ever seen, and they were amazed to find corn and vines growing wild. Leif called this plentiful country Vinland (wine-land). And we now know that it must have been somewhere on the north coast of America.

The Vikings built a camp for shelter. The winter was mild and they were able to cut timber and gather grapes to take back to Greenland. The following spring they set off for home with their cargo.

The discovery of Vinland made Leif's reputation. Several other expeditions were made to his settlement. The Vikings met the local Indians, traded and fought with them.

Trips to Vinland may have continued for hundreds of years. But by the 15th century Greenland had fallen into decay. Its population had been wiped out by cold weather, disease and attacks by Eskimos. Knowledge of Vinland survived only in two Sagas and some remarks in a few manuscripts.

About 500 years after Leif's expedition, Columbus reached America. The discovery astonished Europe, for the Vinland adventure had been completely forgotten.

▲This modern statue of Leif Eriksson is in Iceland. It shows the explorer holding a cross, for he was the first man to bring Christianity to Greenland.

According to the Saga, Leif was "tall and strong and very impressive in appearance. He was a shrewd man and always moderate in his behaviour." He was nicknamed Leif the Lucky.

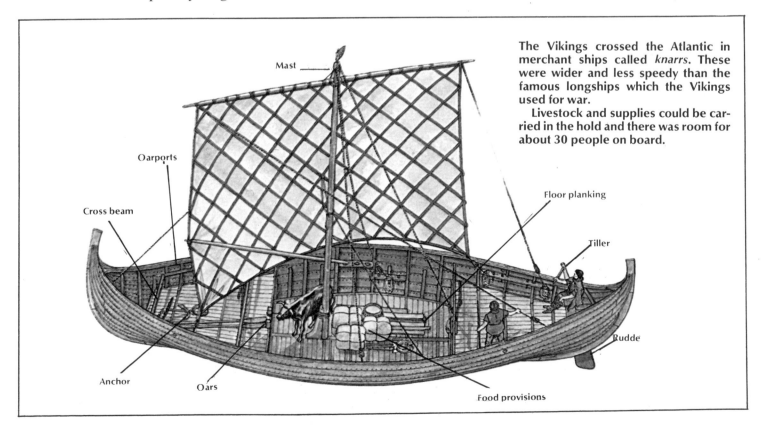

Mast
Oarports
Cross beam
Anchor
Oars
Floor planking
Tiller
Rudder
Food provisions

The Vikings crossed the Atlantic in merchant ships called *knarrs*. These were wider and less speedy than the famous longships which the Vikings used for war.

Livestock and supplies could be carried in the hold and there was room for about 30 people on board.

13

Marco Polo
Exploring the East

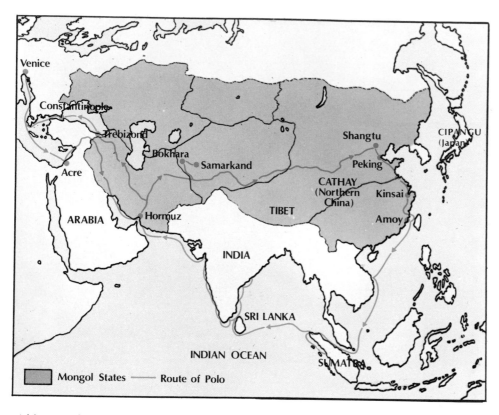

▲Marco Polo's routes to and from Cathay. He also travelled extensively within the Mongol Khan's empire.

▲Marco Polo (c.1253-1324). After his return to Venice, Marco served in the navy and was captured by the Genoese. While in prison he described his travels to a writer called Rustichello.

Marco was nick-named Marco Millions because people believed he exaggerated everything. Many of his tales were only confirmed in the 18th and 19th centuries.

Even in Roman times, Europeans knew that China existed. Traders brought huge quantities of silks from China to Europe across the mountains and deserts of Asia. But the distance was immense, about 10,000 kilometres, and the silks might change hands many times before they reached European markets. No one seems to have had any real idea of what China itself was like. It was known as Serica—the Land of Seres (silkworms).

Then, in 1260, two Venetian merchants called Niccolo and Maffeo Polo made their way eastward, trading in jewels. They travelled in caravans of horses and camels, and their epic journey eventually took them to Peking in Cathay (northern China). As far as we know, they were the first Europeans to set eyes on the city and learn the true splendour of Chinese civilization.

Cathay was then ruled by Kubla Khan, a grandson of Genghis Khan. This fierce Mongol warrior's armies had overrun much of Asia in a whirlwind of destruction. But Kublai Khan was cultured and inquisitive. He treated the Polos courteously and wanted to know more about western ways, particularly about Christianity.

Kublai Khan sent the Polos back on a mission to the Pope. They eventually returned to Cathay after a journey lasting three and a half years. With them came Niccolo's 17-year-old son, Marco, who was staggered by the richness of Cathay. The young man made a good impression on the Khan. He was inquisitive, had a good eye for detail and vivid powers of description. The Khan gave him an official post at his court.

◄ Marco is received by the Great Khan. His palace at Khan-balek (Peking) was "the greatest that ever was" according to Marco. Its walls were covered with gold and silver, and its dining hall alone could seat 6000 people.

▼ Marco described the Chinese way of making paper money. They stripped bark from trees (1), pulped it (2) and mixed it with glue (3). Then they rolled it into flat sheets (4). When dry, it was cut up and stamped it with the Great Khan's seal (5).

The Khan began to send Marco on missions to report on conditions in his great empire. Marco was fascinated by everything, and wrote about what he saw. He described the sprawling capital city, the great river with its fleet of ships. He saw the Chinese making silk, and paper for printed money (which did not exist in Europe).

Marco described Burma and Siam (Thailand), India and Ceylon (Sri Lanka). He saw hill towns perched on high crags in remote Tibet. He spoke of the island of Cipangu (Japan) with its golden temples and pearl fishers. And he also described the northern outposts of the empire, where people rode reindeer and dog sledges, and where polar bears were to be found.

As Kublai Khan grew older, the Polos began to worry that he might die. Perhaps his successor would not be so friendly. So, after 20 years in China, they decided they must leave.

They travelled home by sea, a journey which lasted for two years. When they got back to Venice in 1295 they were almost unrecognizable. They had brought back a fortune in jewels, but no one believed their stories of the Great Khan's empire.

Marco spent the rest of his life as a citizen of Venice, and dictated a full account of his travels to a popular writer. The book sold well, but few people believed that it was based on truth.

It is said that even as Marco lay dying, his friends accused him of lying about his travels. But Marco would not take back one word. "So far from exaggerating," he replied from his deathbed, "I have not told half of what I have seen".

▲ Marco's descriptions were generally very accurate, but early illustrators of his book let their imagination run wild, as this picture shows.

Marco described seeing unicorns. They were "scarcely smaller than elephants... they have a single, large black horn in the middle of the forehead... They are very ugly brutes to look at." Marco was not inventing this; he was clearly describing a rhinoceros.

An Arab Explorer
Ibn Batuta's travels

▲ All Muslims are supposed to make a pilgrimage to Mecca at least once in their lifetime. A pilgrim caravan might be made up of many thousands of people of different races as it converged on the holy city. Poor pilgrims came on foot, others came on camels or horses or were borne on litters.

From the 7th century onwards, the Muslim religion of the Arabs swept the known world in a great arc reaching from North Africa to the borders of China. Christian Europeans feared the mighty Arab Empire. They spoke of all Muslims as Saracens, and considered their religion a threat to civilization.

But the Arabs had a very advanced culture of their own. They set up universities where great advances were made in science, mathematics, astronomy, medicine and geography. They developed great skill as navigators. Even after the Mongols had overrun much of Asia, Muslim influence remained strong.

Ibn Batuta was a learned Arab from Morocco. He developed a passion for travel during a pilgrimage to Mecca (the Muslims' holy city), and visited East Africa, Iran, Arabia and Turkey. But all the time he was attracted by the rich and mysterious continent of India, which he eventually reached in 1333.

He travelled in style, on horse or camel, or carried in a litter surrounded by his servants and slaves. Batuta noted down everything he saw. In the town of Amjhera he watched three Hindu women hurl themselves proudly into the flames of their husband's funeral pyre. In Delhi he saw *yogis* (holy men) perform startling feats of levitation. In Kunakar he met a sultan who rode a white elephant decked out with rubies.

Batuta then passed through the Maldive Islands, which were ruled by a queen. He went to Sri Lanka, was shipwrecked, and then visited Java. Finally, he reached China which impressed him as much as it had Marco Polo. It was he said, "the safest and best regulated of countries for travellers".

During his voyage back to India, Batuta's ship was gripped by a terrible storm. After it had lifted, the sailors claimed to have seen the Great Roc (the giant bird of the Sinbad story). Batuta was not so sure. But he did see something much more terrible when he reached the Middle East. The Black Death had struck. In Damascus 2400 people were dying of the plague *every day*!

Batuta did not return to Morocco until 1349, when he had been away for 24 years. But he soon set off again.

This time he visited Spain, where the Muslims were fighting a holy war against the Christians. Then he returned to North Africa and headed south across the Sahara desert. He visited Timbuktu, heart of a great black empire called Songhai (no European reached it and lived to tell the tale until 500 years later).

Batuta also explored the Niger River, which he thought was part of the Nile. And he heard of a tribe of cannibals who would not eat white men because they thought their flesh "unripe".

Batuta finally returned to Morocco and gave up his wandering ways for good. He spent his last years peacefully in the court of the sultan of Fez. He had visited every Muslim country in the world and many more lands besides. Altogether, he had covered about 120,000 kilometres. He was the greatest traveller of the age.

▲An Arab map of the world, drawn in 1154. If you turn it upside down you can make out the rough outlines of Europe, Asia and North Africa.

▲A modern map showing Ibn Batuta's travels.

►An Arab *dhow*. These boats had huge triangular sails known as "lateens". They allowed Arab navigators to sail with the wind coming at them from many different directions, and were ideal for steering around the gusty coasts of the Indian Ocean. But they were less suitable for long ocean voyages with the wind behind the ship.

Europeans began to add lateen sails to their own ships. Today they are still used in yachting.

▲ Arab navigators used a cross-staff. This instrument was lined up with the midday sun, or a star, to find the height of the sun or star above the horizon. This showed how far north or south the ship was. In modern terms, the cross-staff was used to find the ship's "line of latitude".

17

Columbus
The discovery of the New World

▲Christopher Columbus (c.1451-1506) came from Genoa in Italy, but made his voyages in the service of Spain. He had gone to sea early in life, and studied navigation at Lisbon in Portugal.

From ancient times onwards there had been people who believed that the world was round, so that it should be possible to reach the East by sailing *westward* across the Atlantic. Perhaps India and China, the fabled lands of spices, silks and gold, were only a couple of weeks' sailing from Europe. One Italian adventurer was obsessed by the idea. His name was Christopher Columbus.

By 1492, Columbus had spent many years studying the subject. He had decided that Asia was roughly 4000 kilometres due west of Europe. And he had managed to persuade Queen Isabella of Spain to finance an expedition to prove his theory.

Three ships were provided. On 6 September 1492, they left the Canary Islands and headed west, carrying trinkets for bartering and a letter of introduction to the Great Khan of China.

The ships made good speed. However, in order not to alarm the crews about the distances they were travelling, Columbus pretended that they were going more slowly than they really were.

Only ten days after leaving port, the sailors saw patches of green seaweed in the water. Were they near the coast of Asia already? Columbus was cautious. "I take the mainland to be somewhat further on," he wrote.

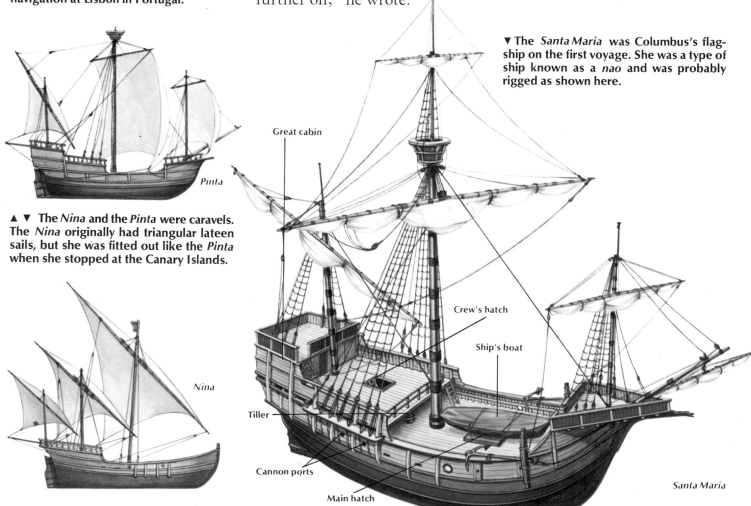

▼ The *Santa Maria* was Columbus's flagship on the first voyage. She was a type of ship known as a *nao* and was probably rigged as shown here.

Pinta

▲ ▼ The *Nina* and the *Pinta* were caravels. The *Nina* originally had triangular lateen sails, but she was fitted out like the *Pinta* when she stopped at the Canary Islands.

Nina

Great cabin

Crew's hatch

Ship's boat

Tiller

Cannon ports

Main hatch

Santa Maria

During the following days they saw weed everywhere, sometimes in great stretches which clogged the ocean. Yet no land was sighted, though there were many false alarms. It was very disturbing. By 10 October the crews were near to mutiny.

The next day, fierce gales lashed at the ships. But when the storm had passed, the sailors saw branches among the waves. Late that night, Columbus thought he saw a light in the distance. And at two in the morning, a sailor sighted land at last!

At daybreak, the explorers headed for the small green island that lay ahead. They waded ashore, to a beach crowded with astonished natives. The Spaniards offered them trinkets, and the natives gave the sailors parrots, cotton and spears in return. Columbus believed he had reached Asia at last, and called the islanders "Indians".

He had made one of the greatest voyages, and greatest mistakes, in the history of exploration. He did not realize that he had reached the island fringe of a vast new continent: America.

Columbus explored the islands and set up a fort. Then, leaving men behind to guard it, he returned to Spain. He declared that he had found a way to the East and was greeted as a hero.

Columbus made three more trips to the "Indies", built settlements and eventually set foot on the mainland of America. But there was little gold to be found. The explorer managed his settlements badly and was even punished by being put in irons for a while.

Though other explorers were beginning to realize that he had discovered a New World, Columbus refused to accept it. He died in 1506, a bitter man, still denying the existence of the great continent that he had discovered.

▲ Columbus is sent back to Spain in chains in 1500, after mismanaging his colonies on Hispaniola (modern Haiti).

He had tortured and enslaved the Indians while trying to extract gold from the population. But Queen Isabella pardoned him and he set out on his fourth voyage two years later.

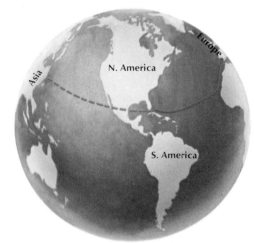

▲ By Columbus's time most mapmakers knew that the world was round rather than flat. Columbus had no idea of the size of the globe, however. He believed that it was roughly 4000 kilometres from Europe to Asia.

In fact, the distance is about 19,000 kilometres, and America lies between them.

Cortés the Conqueror
The Spaniards in Mexico

▼ The Aztec city of Tenochtitlan was built on an island in Lake Texcoco. There were few roads, and boats were used for getting about on the canals.

The main square was vast, and held 60,000 people on market days. There was a palace, school, ball court and temples. Modern Mexico City is built on the ruins of Tenochtitlan.

In August 1519 Hernando Cortés led his small army inland from the hot, unhealthy swamplands of the Mexican coast. There were some 500 Spaniards, fifteen horses and six cannons. They climbed high into the volcanic peaks of Mexico's mountain ranges. For somewhere in the unknown interior there was rumoured to be a great city rich in gold and silver. This was Tenochtitlan, the capital of the mighty Aztec Empire.

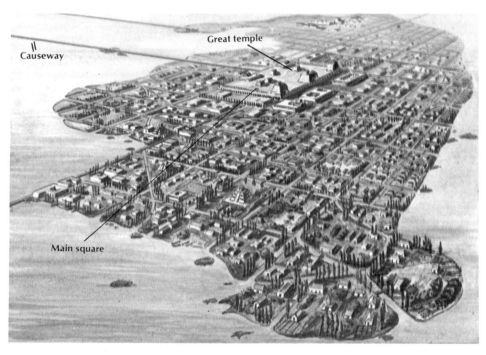

Causeway

Great temple

Main square

▲ Hernando Cortés (1485-1547) migrated to the New World from Spain in 1504. After conquering the Aztecs (1519-21) he became the Governor of Mexico and launched three expeditions to explore Central America. He died a wealthy man owning vast estates.

▲ A Mexican gold mask. The Spaniards melted down hundreds of similar articles. An Aztec wrote, "They longed and lusted for gold. Their bodies swelled with greed and their hunger was ravenous; they hungered like pigs for that gold." Few examples of Aztec goldwork remain.

◄ An Aztec picture showing a battle with the Spaniards. The Aztec warriors wore fantastic costumes of animal skins and featherwork, but they were no match for the Spanish guns and cavalry.

► The Aztecs practised human sacrifice on a massive scale. They would tear the hearts from live victims as offerings to their gods. Captive Spaniards were sacrificed in this way during the siege of Tenochtitlan.

The Spanish *conquistadors* (conquerors) battle with the Aztecs in the streets of Tenochtitlan.

The Spaniards had already glimpsed something of Aztec civilization. They had seen towns built of stone, pyramids and temples much more majestic than the primitive villages Columbus had discovered. They had marched through abandoned settlements where human hearts lay piled on altars dripping with blood, the gory remains of human sacrifice, practised by the Aztec priests.

At first the local mountain peoples fought the Spaniards. But they hated the Aztecs and later agreed to march with the Spaniards towards Tenochtitlan.

Meanwhile, Montezuma, the Aztec ruler, was growing nervous. He had heard reports of these pale-faced strangers with their terrifying guns and cavalry (the Aztecs had never seen horses or firearms before). He tried to bribe them not to come further by sending gifts of gold and fine cloth.

The Spaniards were also uneasy. Montezuma was said to have 150,000 warriors. The odds against the explorers were enormous. On 7 November, having marched for 400 kilometres, they reached the great lakes from which the Aztec capital arose. The sight was breathtaking. A soldier wrote, "these great towns and pyramids and buildings rising from the water, all made of stone, seemed like an enchanted vision".

They trooped down the causeway that led to the city. The lake swarmed with canoes. Pavements and rooftops were thronged with thousands of inhabitants eager to glimpse the invaders. Chieftains in brilliant robes came to pay homage. At last, the great Montezuma himself arrived beneath a canopy of green feathers worked in gold, silver and pearls. He welcomed the Spaniards as gods.

The explorers were given sumptuous living quarters at the palace. One day they found Montezuma's treasure hoard in a secret room, stole it and divided the spoils among themselves.

Cortés had discovered an empire of great splendour and great barbarity, ruled by a man who was proud but superstitious. He seems to have believed that the Spaniards were followers of the Aztec god Quetzalcoatl, come to claim his kingdom. Montezuma let himself be taken prisoner in his own palace. He was eventually killed by his own people, who then drove the Spaniards out.

But Cortés soon returned with reinforcements and laid siege to the city. In the slaughter that followed, Tenochtitlan was razed to the ground. The "enchanted vision" became a place of death, and Aztec civilization died with it.

Magellan
Around the world

"We are about to enter an ocean where no ship has ever sailed before," said Magellan. "May the sea always be as calm and benevolent as it is today. In this hope, I name it the Pacific Ocean [ocean of peace]." The date was 28 November 1520, and Magellan's dream had come true. He had at last found a way round the southern tip of America to the uncharted sea beyond.

The previous year Magellan had set out from Spain with five ships. One had been wrecked off the coast of South America. Another had deserted the fleet and returned to Spain. But the three remaining ships, *Trinidad*, *Concepcion* and *Vittoria*, had passed through the narrow straits at the tip of the continent.

Now, Magellan believed, the rich Spice Islands of the East were only a few days' sailing away. The little fleet headed north-west across the vast Pacific. Days passed, then weeks. At every moment the explorers expected to see the mainland of Asia looming on the horizon. They had no idea of the immensity of the ocean that lay ahead.

Food began to run out. The last provisions became infested with maggots, the drinking water grew foul. Then the disease of scurvy appeared, swelling the sailors' joints, rotting their gums and covering their bodies with sores. After six weeks, men began to die.

Those who survived were so weak they could hardly walk and only a handful had enough strength to man the rigging. It seemed they were doomed to sail across the empty ocean until death claimed them all.

▲ Ferdinand Magellan (1470-1521) was a Portuguese navigator. He was disliked by the King of Portugal, so he offered his services to Spain.

He set off to reach the Spice Islands (the Moluccas) with five ships, and twice had to put down mutinies headed by his own commanders before he even set sail across the Pacific Ocean.

◄ Magellan's three ships pass through the narrow seaway which still bears his name: the Magellan Straits.

◄ Magellan's three ships pass through the narrow seaway which still bears his name: the Magellan Straits.

Navigating this stormy channel was a great achievement in itself. Now the little fleet faced the challenge of the mighty Pacific Ocean.

▼ The riches of the East were a lure which attracted many explorers to brave uncharted oceans. Columbus and Magellan both sailed westward. In 1497-9 the Portuguese navigator, Vasco da Gama, found an easterly sea-route around the southern tip of Africa.

Magellan was not seeking a source of gold, but of spices such as pepper, cinnamon, nutmeg, ginger and cloves. These were immensely valuable to the Europeans of his day. They used them to disguise the taste of the food, since it could not be kept fresh for long.

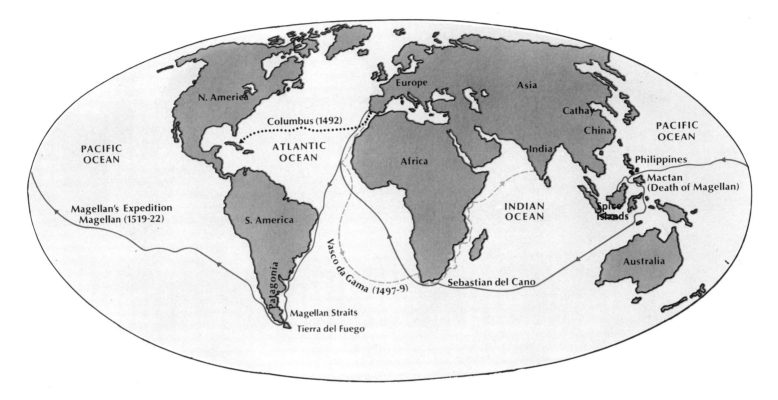

▲ A Portuguese map of the Magellan Straits, made after the voyage. Magellan called the land further south Tierra del Fuego (Land of the Fires).

Was it the tip of another continent? Sir Francis Drake proved it was just an island when he led the second voyage round the world in 1577-80 in his flagship, the *Golden Hinde*.

Then, on 25 January, hope returned. The explorers sighted an island. It was deserted, but at least it had fresh water, with fish, crabs and turtles' eggs. They rested for some days to get back their health, then sailed on, confident that Asia was near.

But only one other deserted island came into view. Again, sailors fell sick and died. Again, weeks passed on the deserted sea. On 4 March, Magellan handed out the last rations: a few mouldy biscuits crumbled up and mixed with sawdust.

Two days later a starving seaman went aloft to scan the ocean yet again. A great wooded island was quite close by! Twice he opened his mouth but could make not a sound. But on a third attempt he managed to yell, "Praise God! Land! Land!"

The starving sailors wept and laughed. Natives in canoes came swarming around the ships. At last, the explorers had crossed the mighty Pacific and reached the Far East.

But the voyage ended tragically. Magellan was killed in a battle with some Philippine islanders he was trying to convert to Christianity. The other members of the expedition turned to piracy. They scuttled the *Concepcion*. The *Trinidad's* crew were captured and hung as pirates by the Portuguese.

Alone, the *Vittoria* sailed on, finally returning to Spain three years after the expedition had set out. Of the 277 men and five ships only one ship and nineteen men had come back. But those nineteen men had achieved a stupendous feat. They were the first people to sail right round the world.

Down the Amazon
Orellana's voyage

In 1540, a Spanish expedition led by Gonzalo Pizarro set out from Quito (in modern Ecuador). Its aim was to explore the forests beyond the great Andes mountains. Here Pizarro was hoping to find a land as rich as Aztec Mexico, or Inca Peru.

The 220 Spaniards who set out were accompanied by 4000 Indian slaves, with dogs, horses and llamas as pack animals. Hundreds of the party died crossing the Andes. But when the rest reached the rain-forests beyond, they found no golden cities. The poor local tribes knew nothing of any treasure. Pizarro was enraged and had some of them burnt alive, others torn apart by dogs.

The Indians quickly learnt how to get rid of the treasure-seekers. Yes, they said, further ahead lay regions rich in gold. And the explorers left, marching deeper into the jungle.

Food was scarce and men died of fever. When they reached the Napo River, Pizarro ordered a halt. The explorers built a ship to carry their sick and baggage, then pressed on. Still they found no gold. Finally, Pizarro sent his second-in-command, Francisco de Orellana, to sail downstream and seek provisions. And so, with 57 companions, Orellana set off.

He did not come back. Believing Orellana had deliberately deserted the party, Pizarro led the ragged survivors of his expedition back to Quito. The search for gold had ended in disaster.

What *had* happened to Orellana? It seems that he had been carried downstream by the current, his men too weak to row back. They drifted for days, finding no food, until they were forced to eat snakes and toads, even their belts and shoe-leather, boiled with plants. All around loomed the dark jungle, where strange birds shrieked and monkeys chattered.

At last, the explorers came upon an Indian tribe who gave them food and protection through their waters. The Spaniards drifted downstream and were carried, unknown to themselves, into the largest river in the world. They built a second boat, a sailing ship known as a brigantine, and headed onwards while the great river swelled with every tributary they passed.

Once, they were chased by 5000 hostile tribesmen in war canoes. Once they sailed through the territory of a head-hunting tribe where shrunken heads grinned at them from the banks.

In June, the explorers fought a fierce battle with a tribe they thought was made up entirely of warlike women. Remembering the female warriors of Greek myths, they spoke of them as Amazons. From this incident, the mighty river gained its name: the Amazon.

At last, the explorers reached the river's mouth, where colossal ocean waves crashed against their ship. But the sturdy little craft survived, ploughing through the turbulent delta to the calmer waters of the open sea. Eventually, they reached Trinidad.

Orellana had led his men right down the Amazon, from one of its sources to the sea, a journey of about 5000 kilometres. And in doing so he had crossed the South American continent.

▲ The Amazon basin encloses more than 4 million square kilometres of dense forest which was entirely unknown in Orellana's time.

▲ Orellana's route. The explorers made their first boat using nails from their horse-shoes, and gum from trees for pitch. Yet the little craft sailed the full length of the Amazon.

WILDLIFE OF THE AMAZON

The wildlife of the Amazon includes strange and exotic creatures such as the saki monkey (left) and the keel-billed toucan (below).

Beneath the explorers' boats swarmed shoals of flesh-eating piranha, fish which can strip the flesh from a body in a matter of seconds.

▼ It took the explorers 35 days to build their second boat, using materials supplied by Indians. Sails made from blankets were used on the way to Trinidad.

> "*These women are very white and tall, and have very long hair, braided and wound about the head. They go about naked but with their privy parts covered. With their bows and arrows in their hands, they do as much fighting as ten Indian men.*"
> *FRIAR CARVAJAL*

▲ A monk called Friar Carvajal accompanied Orellana and wrote an account of the journey.

He described a tribe of fierce women warriors who were referred to as Amazons. Did they really exist? Most historians believe that the friar was exaggerating

Perhaps the Amazons were just a tribe of long-haired male warriors, with a few women among them.

The explorers fought off many native attacks. Orellana lost an eye in one encounter. In another, the natives fired arrows tipped with deadly *curare* poison.

La Salle

Down the Mississipp

▲ **René Robert de La Salle (1643-87)** From 1669 to 1681 he made several expeditions to explore the Great Lakes and the upper waters of the Mississippi. Backed by the French Government, he built forts and traded in furs.

Travelling among the warlike Huron and Iroquois Indians was dangerous. Another young French explorer, Etienne Brulé, was killed and eaten by the Hurons.

The French were the most energetic explorers in Canada. Trappers, traders and missionary priests penetrated the St Lawrence River and the Great Lakes. They learnt of the Mississippi, a huge, south-flowing river which the Indians called the Great Water. And they had begun to explore its upper reaches.

In 1669, a young fur trader called René de La Salle set off into the backwoods to explore the pine forests surrounding the Great Lakes. Sometimes, Indians who turned up at French trading posts would speak of this solitary white man wandering among them, learning their languages and making friends with the tribes.

Three years later he returned with a great plan. He believed it must be possible to sail down the Mississippi to the Gulf of Mexico. And he dreamed of claiming the whole river valley for Louis XIV of France. The territory would be enormous: bounded in the west by the Rocky Mountains, in the east by the Appalachians, in the north by the Great Lakes and the south by the sea.

La Salle went to France twice to get official backing. Then he led an expedition which set up a network of forts between the Great Lakes and the Illinois River (which flowed into the Mississippi). Finally, he gathered a party of 23 Frenchmen and 18 Mohican and Abenaki Indians, with their squaws and children. The aim was to sail the Great Water to the southern coastlands which had already been explored by Spanish adventurers.

They set off in December 1680, dragging their birchbark canoes on sledges down nearly 200 kilometres of frozen river. Then they were able to launch their craft and paddle downstream.

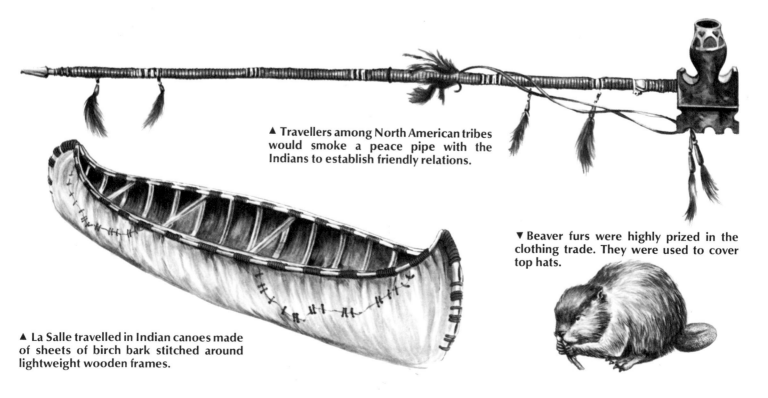

▲ Travellers among North American tribes would smoke a peace pipe with the Indians to establish friendly relations.

▼ Beaver furs were highly prized in the clothing trade. They were used to cover top hats.

▲ La Salle travelled in Indian canoes made of sheets of birch bark stitched around lightweight wooden frames.

▲ La Salle claims Louisiana for the King of France (a 19th century print).

The weather grew warmer. Pine forests gave way to broad, rolling prairies where herds of buffalo roamed. This was the heartland of North America. The explorers met no serious opposition, and local Indian tribes often greeted them with dancing and festivities. At each village, La Salle would set up a wooden cross, fire a salute and claim the land and its peoples for King Louis.

At last, the explorers reached the swampy delta of the Mississippi, where they saw alligators lounging on the banks. Reaching the sea, La Salle laid claim to the whole river valley.

La Salle then made his way back upriver. Eventually he returned to France, where he was proclaimed Governor of Louisiana, as the vast new territory was called. He was given four ships, settlers and supplies to set up a colony at the mouth of the Mississippi.

But when he arrived in the Gulf of Mexico, La Salle could not find the river mouth. By mistake, he had sailed 640 kilometres too far west. Two ships returned to France but the other two were wrecked. His small party was stranded on the barren Texas coast.

La Salle searched for the Mississippi without success. Then he led the surviving members of his party north towards Canada. Sick and exhausted, his followers mutinied. And René de La Salle, the empire-builder, was shot dead by one of his own men.

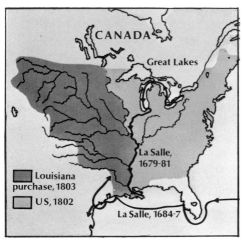

▲ La Salle's route down the Mississippi, and the disastrous voyage which led to his death.

Louisiana remained in French hands until 1803. Then Napoleon sold it to the newly formed United States for only 15 million dollars, roughly four cents an acre. The United States doubled in area overnight.

27

Captain Cook

In search of the Southern Continent

On 13 July 1770, Lieutenant James Cook sailed his ship *Endeavour* away from the Pacific island of Tahiti. From here, scientists on board had been making observations of the planet Venus. The crew and passengers believed their work was over.

But it was not yet time to return to England. Cook was carrying secret orders from the British Admiralty. Now he opened a sealed envelope and announced the true purpose of the expedition. They were to sail in search of a rich Southern Continent.

Most mapmakers assumed that there must a great continent in the south to balance the land mass of Asia in the north. Australia had been discovered by the Dutch, and the explorer Abel Tasman had sailed around it, proving that it was not attached to any southern land mass. However, Tasman had only seen the west coast of New Zealand. Was this the tip of the unknown continent?

Cook's mission was to find out. He set course for New Zealand, and reached its east coast. Despite battles with fierce Maori warriors, he managed to sail right round the land, charting every bay and headland. Cook found that New Zealand was made up of two islands. Neither was connected to any continent.

Cook then sailed west, reached Australia and worked his way up the coast, methodically mapping as he went. At one point, his ship struck the jagged coral of the Great Barrier Reef, and only Cook's brilliant seamanship saved her.

While the *Endeavour* was being repaired inshore, the crew saw a strange creature. It went "only upon two legs, making vast bounds". They were the first Europeans to see a kangaroo.

Cook came home in 1771, having sailed around the world. The next year he set off again to settle the question of the Southern Continent once and for all. He got further south than anyone had been before and crossed the Antarctic Circle. He turned back only when his path was blocked by dense pack-ice.

Cook sailed round the world in the southern sea and found that the Great Continent did not exist. But he concluded, rightly, that there might be some ice-bound land around the South Pole.

In 1776, Cook set out on a third great voyage. He discovered the Hawaiian islands and charted the Bering Strait between Asia and America. Then he entered the Arctic Sea, seeking an eastward route to the Atlantic, only to find his path blocked by ice.

He returned to Hawaii to take on supplies. Then disaster struck. A fight broke out between some of his men and some islanders and, during the violence, Cook was stabbed and clubbed to death.

His death was particularly tragic, for he had always treated the native peoples he met with kindness and respect. He also cared for his sailors; he insisted on cleanliness in their quarters, and made them eat fresh vegetables to prevent attacks of scurvy. With his death, the world had lost more than a brilliant navigator. It had also lost an explorer of great humanity.

▲ James Cook (1728-79) began his career as a surveyor of the St Lawrence River. He came from a poor farming family and achieved fame only by his own efforts.

◄ A model of the *Endeavour*. She was built as a collier (coal-ship) and was converted for Cook's expedition. Ten new cabins were built, so that the ship could hold nearly a hundred men. Her flat bottom made her easier to steer round shallow reefs and uncharted coasts.

► An 18th-century sextant, of the type used by Cook for surveying coasts. Like the earlier cross-staff, it was used for finding lines of latitude, but was a much more precise instrument. When combined with a chronometer, it could be used to find lines of longitude (see page 46).

▼ War canoes in Tahiti, preparing for an attack on the nearby island of Moorea. The picture was painted by William Hodges, one of Cook's official artists. Explorers used artists as modern travellers use photographers.

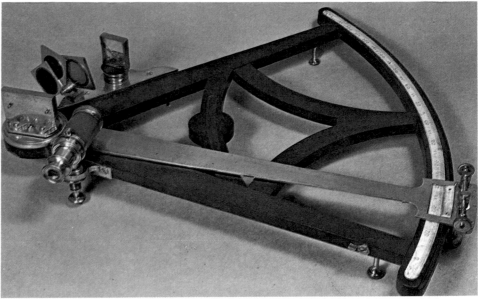

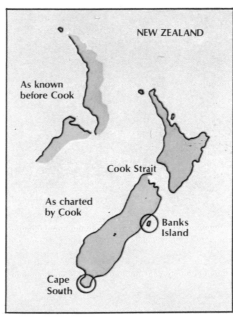

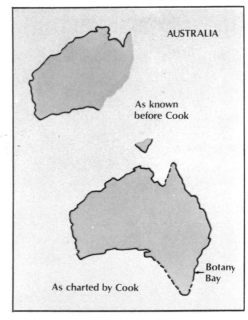

▲ Cook was a brilliant mapmaker. These pictures show New Zealand and Australia as known before and after Cook.

In charting New Zealand, Cook made only two serious mistakes. His "Cape South" is really an island called Stewart Island. And what he called "Banks Island" is really a peninsula.

The point at which he reached Australia was so rich in plant life that he named it Botany Bay.

◄ Cook's death on Hawaii. Some of the natives began to steal from his ships, and a quarrel arose. His men opened fire. Cook went ashore and told them to stop shooting. While his back was turned, he was stabbed and clubbed to death in the shallows.

When he died, a sailor wrote that "we all felt that we had lost a father."

The White Mountain
The conquest of Mont Blanc

"I could not even look upon the mountain without being seized by an aching desire," wrote Horace De Saussure. He was describing Mont Blanc, the highest mountain in Europe. In the heart of civilized Europe lay regions where no human foot had ever trodden: the snow-covered ridges and peaks of the Alps.

Mountaineering as we know it today did not exist in the 18th century. It was begun by De Saussure, a Swiss scientist who was fascinated by the plant life, atmospheric conditions and rock formations of the Alps. From 1773 onwards he made frequent trips to the area. Again and again he saw the white dome of Mont Blanc towering above him. The summit was 4734 metres above sea-level and he longed to know what conditions were like at that height.

◄ **Horace De Saussure (1740-1799), a Swiss scientist who taught at the academy in Geneva. His interests included geology, physics, chemistry and botany.**

A few enthusiasts (including the mediaeval Italian poet, Petrarch) had scaled peaks before. But mountaineering did not exist as a true sport.

► **Mont Blanc (the White Mountain) whose summit is the highest point in Europe. Local peasants had ventured around its lower slopes, but none had dared approach the upper reaches. Superstitious villagers even believed that goblins and monsters haunted the heights.**

▼ **De Saussure's expedition makes its way up the mountain. The guides carried sacks of instruments for taking scientific readings. Notice the spiked shoes, specially designed by De Saussure to give a better grip when climbing over snow and ice.**

De Saussure offered a reward to the first person who would find a route to the top. Many attempts were made, but the adventurers were repeatedly driven back by walls of ice, rumbling avalanches and deep crevasses in the glaciers which grind their way down the mountain's slopes.

However, one local doctor kept trying. His name was Michel Paccard and on 7 August 1786 he set out yet again. With him went a local deer-hunter called Jacques Balmat.

They started in the afternoon. By nightfall they had reached Montagne de la Côte on the lower slopes. Here they camped for the night. The next morning they began their assault on the summit. They had neither ropes nor icepicks, only their *alpenstocks*, the long, pointed walking-sticks used by all Alpine travellers.

The explorers made their way across a broad ice-field. Sometimes they had to crawl on their hands and knees. Black crevasses yawned all around them. Then they struggled over a jagged rocky ridge. Beyond it lay two plateaus where they waded through waist-deep drifts of powdery snow. Further ahead was a steep, icy slope and two more ridges of rock.

Evening was beginning to fall. Both men had frostbite. They had to fight for every breath in the thin mountain air. Yet, step by step, they urged themselves on. At 6.30 pm they reached the summit.

The light was failing as they began their descent, and a full moon rose above the snow. They marched down through the night, reached Chamonix the next day and announced their great achievement.

De Saussure gave the promised reward to Balmat (Paccard was not interested in the money). And the next year the scientist followed their path to the summit. He took 18 guides to carry his scientific equipment. The thinness of the air forced them down again after only four hours. Later, De Saussure set up a scientific base on the nearby Col du Géant.

The expeditions received enormous publicity and started a craze for mountaineering which has never died down. Less than 200 years later, every major peak in the world has been scaled.

Heinrich Barth
A German explorer in Africa

To European explorers, the Sahara desert at first seemed an impenetrable barrier. Yet caravans had long been crossing its sandy wastes, carrying salt, gold and slaves between the African interior and the Arab states to the north. One of the first Europeans to follow the trade routes was the German, Heinrich Barth.

In 1850, Barth set out with a caravan from Tripoli, making detailed notes as he went. He studied the Tuareg nomads, who controlled trade across the desert. This proud "people of the veil" jealously guarded their secrets and often robbed and killed travellers.

Barth also explored the Sahara's mountain ranges and discovered ancient rock paintings in the heart of the desert. These showed that many people and animals had once lived there.

Beyond the Sahara, Barth travelled through the bushlands of North West Africa, exploring in a great sweep from Lake Chad to Timbuktu. Here there were ancient black empires and thriving towns where Arabs and Africans had mingled for centuries.

Barth wanted to open up the area for European merchants. He also hoped that European influence would end the slave trade. But he treated both Arabs and Africans with respect and mixed freely with the people. He was quite unlike the Christians described by one Fulani tribesman as "sitting like women in the bottom of their steamboats and doing nothing but eating raw eggs".

▲ Heinrich Barth (1821-65). The German explorer won respect after his first expedition to North Africa and the Middle East in 1845-7.

The great expedition of 1850-55 was backed by the British Government. His two companions, Richardson and Overweg, died during the trip.

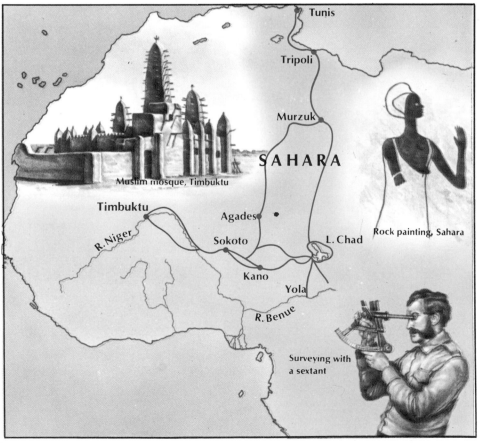

Muslim mosque, Timbuktu

Rock painting, Sahara

Surveying with a sextant

◄ A slave caravan crosses the Sahara. Arab traders would make raids on African villages in the interior and return across the Sahara. Men, women and children were shackled and driven like animals to Arab slave markets.

▼ A Tuareg nomad today. Tuaregs called themselves the Lords of the Desert and operated the trans-Saharan caravans. Alexandrine Tinné, a young Dutch woman explorer, was killed by Tuaregs in 1869.

> "*I looked long and silently upon the stream; it was one of the happiest moments of my life.*"
>
> *HEINRICH BARTH,*
> *18 JUNE, 1851*

▲ Barth describes his first sighting of the River Benue, the eastern branch of the mighty Niger River. Barth was the first European to set eyes on the Benue's upper reaches.

◄ Barth's routes during his 1850-55 expedition across the Sahara and through North West Africa.

He discovered ancient rock paintings in the Sahara (this one shows a Fulbe girl of about 2000-3000 BC).

Barth drew meticulous maps, took constant sightings and kept a full daily register of weather conditions.

Timbuktu was a great Muslim centre of trade and learning. It was jealously protected from white explorers and became a city of great mystery. The first European to reach it and live to tell the tale was a Frenchman, René Caillié (1827). Like Barth and other later explorers, he disguised himself as an Arab.

Barth travelled by horse or camel, buying protection from the local rulers with European goods. He gave so many needles to the Hausa people that they called him the Needle Prince.

In some places it was dangerous to be known as a Christian, so Barth used the Arab name of Abd el Karim and often disguised himself as an Arab. He even stained his face dark brown on one occasion. But his disguises were useless in the fiercely Muslim city of Timbuktu. Barth was kept virtually prisoner there for six months for fear of being murdered as soon as he got beyond the city walls.

Like all explorers in Africa, Barth suffered frequent attacks of fever. Other perils included hordes of white ants which once devoured his leather bags.

Thieves were a constant menace. One night, African tribesmen stole his Arab companion's blanket with the Arab still clinging to it! Barth fired shots into the air and spent the night loudly playing the accordion: "I frightened the people to such a degree that they thought we were about to ransack the town."

Barth was the most accurate mapmaker of all the explorers in Africa. He was also the first true historian of the African states, and a brilliant linguist. After a hard day's travelling, he might sit for hours learning the vocabulary of the local tribe.

But despite his achievements, Barth never became a popular hero. His return to Europe in 1855 was not even mentioned in the newspapers. He died ten years later, of a stomach complaint. He was only 44: a great explorer almost unknown to the public.

Burke and Wills
Across Australia

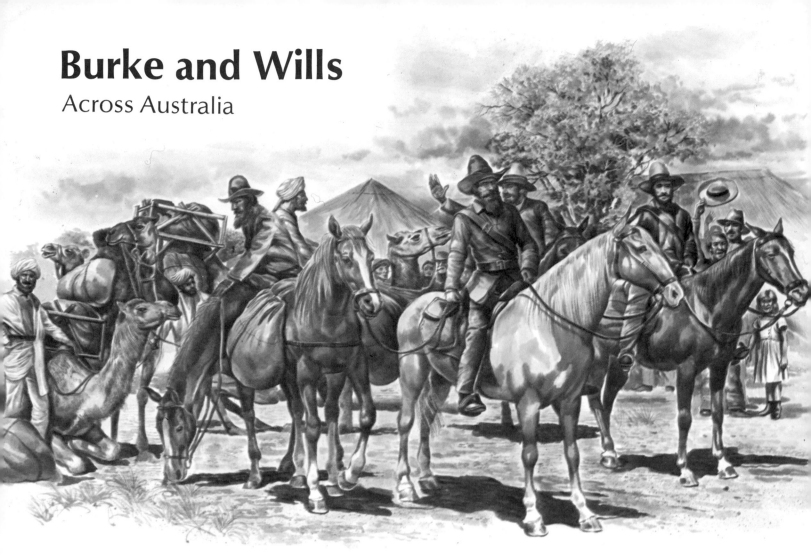

▲ The expedition sets out from Melbourne on 20 August, 1860. Three Indian soldiers looked after the camels. The pack animals carried 180 kilograms of supplies: tents, tools, scientific instruments. Food and drink included flour, rice, oatmeal, dried meat, lime juice; and 250 litres of rum for the camels!

Burke

Wills

▲ Robert Burke (1820-61), the Irish-Australian leader of the expedition, had been a police inspector. He was a brave but hot-headed man, and had no experience of mounting an expedition. W.J. Wills was his second-in-command.

On 11 February 1861, Robert Burke and William Wills struggled wearily into the swamps of the Gulf of Carpentaria. At last they had achieved their goal. They had become the first men to cross Australia from south to north.

Eighteen men had set out from Melbourne six months before. It was a big expedition, with pack-horses and 26 imported camels to carry their baggage across the desert.

Some members of the party had been delayed during the early stages. Others were camped at depots along the route. Only Burke and Wills actually reached the north coast. And now, already exhausted, they began to retrace their steps.

After a couple of days they reached the camp where two companions, John King and Charles Gray, were waiting. Then the four men trudged back together to a big depot at Cooper's Creek. Heavy rains began to fall. The going was slow. One after another their camels were slaughtered for meat.

Then Gray fell sick and died. Only one thought kept the others going as they limped onwards. At Cooper's Creek their companions were waiting with food, fresh horses and camels.

On the evening of 21 April they finally reached the depot. Burke fired three shots in the air as a greeting. Oddly, no shots were fired in reply. The explorers hurried into the camp. It was deserted. The huge food store was gone. From a message left at the camp, they learnt that their companions had started for Melbourne that same day, believing they were dead!

The three men could never catch their companions up. Their camels were exhausted and their own legs were aching with cramp.

A few provisions had been left. Taking them, Burke, Wills and King headed towards a lonely cattle station where they knew there would be food. But their way led through a scorching desert. In despair, they turned back to Cooper's Creek.

Now their provisions had run out. They shot a few birds and gathered some seeds, but this meagre diet could not sustain them. They began to starve. A tribe of Aborigines had been watching their collapse and seemed anxious to help. But Burke was nervous and stupidly fired his pistol to scare them off.

On 28 June Wills scrawled in his diary, "my pulse is at 48, my legs and arms are skin and bone. I am very weak . . ." Two days later he was dead. Then Burke collapsed too. King cradled him in his arms until he passed away. In the distance, the watching Aborigines wept. Now King staggered alone into the desert.

When their companions reached Melbourne, they sent back search parties to look for the lost leaders of the expedition. A party met some Aborigines near Cooper's Creek. As they approached, most of the natives fled. But one remained, a wild figure with skin tanned black by the sun. It was King.

John King had been looked after by the Aborigines for about a month, and survived the tragedy. But all that was found of Burke and Wills was a handful of bones which were brought back to Melbourne for a state funeral.

▲ The three weary explorers reach Cooper's Creek. Their companions had carved a message on a tree saying "Dig 3ft. N.W." At this spot, Burke found a buried message saying that they had left that very day with "six camels and twelve horses in good working condition."

▲ The route of Burke and Wills. They set out to cross 2400 kilometres of territory which was almost completely unknown. It was rumoured that rich and fertile regions lay inland.

Livingstone
Exploring Africa

▲ David Livingstone (1813-73), the Scottish doctor, first went to Africa in 1840 as a missionary. He was convinced that Christianity would only take root if the Arab slave trade was abolished and European merchants penetrated the so-called Dark Continent.

▶ In 1844, Livingstone was attacked by a wounded lion which gashed his arm, splintering the bone. The explorer was saved in the nick of time by an African companion. But afterwards Livingstone could never raise his left arm higher than his shoulder.

▶ During Livingstone's second great expedition (1852-6) he crossed Africa from coast to coast and discovered a mighty waterfall on the Zambezi. The Africans called it Mosioatunya (the smoke that thunders). Livingstone named it the Victoria Falls.

Where was Doctor Livingstone? For years, no European had set eyes on the explorer. He was known to be somewhere in the heart of Africa, but where exactly? Was he alive or dead?

David Livingstone was a Scottish doctor and missionary who had become a hero to Victorian Britain. He was the first European to cross central Africa from coast to coast. He had explored the Zambezi River and discovered the Victoria Falls. He had also revealed the horrors of the Arab and Portuguese slave trade.

In 1866, Livingstone had set out on his last expedition. He wanted to learn more about the trade in slaves. He also wanted to find the source of the Nile, Africa's greatest river.

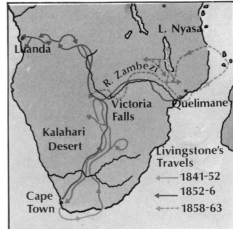

▲ Livingstone penetrated deep into Africa in his second and third expeditions (1852-6 and 1858-63). On the third journey he discovered Lake Nyasa.

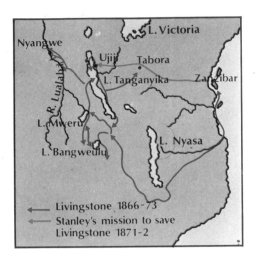

▼ Livingstone's last expedition in search of the source of the Nile (1865-73); and Stanley's 1000-kilometre journey to find him.

Nyangwe
L. Victoria
Ujiji · Tabora
L. Tanganyika · Zanzibar
R. Lualaba
L. Mweru
L. Bangweulu
L. Nyasa

⟵ Livingstone 1866-73
⟵ Stanley's mission to save Livingstone 1871-2

Livingstone was travelling on foot, with only a handful of African servants. Soon the outside world lost track of him and rumours spread that he was dead.

In fact, Livingstone was not dead, but he was very ill. He had spent months exploring the area around Lake Tanganyika, wading waist deep through endless swamps. He was stricken by fever. "Excessively weak, cannot walk without tottering, constant singing in my head," he noted at one point. Finally, he stopped at a settlement called Ujiji, his strength almost gone.

Meanwhile, an American newspaper, the *New York Herald*, had sent a journalist called H. M. Stanley to Africa to find Livingstone. In January 1871, Stanley set out from Zanzibar with a party of 200 African porters, with their wives and cattle.

The expedition made its way through steaming coastal jungles and over higher grasslands raging with tribal war. Stanley himself collapsed with fever several times. But, by autumn 1872, the party was close to Ujiji and heard rumours that there was a grey-bearded white man in the town ahead.

On 10 November 1872, the explorers reached Ujiji. Crowds of Africans surrounded Stanley's party and a thin, half-starved figure emerged from a hut to greet him.

It was Livingstone. The months of searching were over. Stanley was suddenly overcome by shyness in the presence of the great man. He walked rather stiffly up to him, took off his hat and said simply, "Doctor Livingstone, I presume".

Stanley's arrival with food and supplies gave Livingstone a new lease of life. The two men became friends and spent four months exploring Lake Tanganyka together. But when Stanley returned to the coast, Livingstone decided to stay.

Livingstone continued his search for the source of the Nile alone. He never found it. About a year later, he died in the swamps of Bangweulu.

But Livingstone's hopes did not die. As a result of his efforts, the British government persuaded the Sultan of Zanzibar to close his slave market. In the year of Livingstone's death, the last slave was sold publicly on the East African coast.

▲ "Doctor Livingstone, I presume." The famous meeting between Livingstone and Stanley at Ujiji.

Stanley later became a great explorer in his own right. In 1874-7 he made a hazardous journey across Africa from the coast of modern Tanzania to the mouth of the Congo. Unlike Livingstone, he travelled with an army of 353 native porters.

▲ By April 1873, Livingstone was too weak to walk. His African servants carried him in a litter through the swamps of Bangweulu, where he finally died.

His followers buried his heart in the soil of central Africa, then carried his body back to the coast. It now lies in Westminster Abbey in London.

The Race for the Pole

Scott and Amundsen

▼ Robert Falcon Scott (1868-1912) in his Antarctic base at McMurdo Sound. From 1901 to 1904 he made his first expedition to Antarctica in his ship *Discovery* and organized several long sledge trips inland. On one journey he got within 80 kilometres of the Pole.

"Only twenty-seven miles [43 kilometres] from the Pole. We ought to do it now," wrote Captain Scott. It was the evening of 15 January 1912. Scott and his four companions, Oates, Wilson, Evans and Bowers, lay huddled in their tent. Outside, the Antarctic night was bitterly cold. But the explorers had made good time that day. Now they believed they would certainly reach the South Pole.

Only one worry disturbed their thoughts. They knew that the Norwegian explorer, Roald Amundsen, was also making a dash for the pole. Who would reach it first?

Scott and his companions felt fairly confident. On 16 January they dragged their sledges swiftly on, throughout the morning. But in the afternoon they saw a black speck ahead. They urged themselves forward, and found to their horror that it was a flag, used for marking a route. The area was covered with paw-marks and sledge-tracks. Amundsen's team had already passed this way with their lightweight dog-sledges.

It was a bitter disappointment. A Force 5 gale lashed their faces as they surveyed the desolate snowscape. "Great God!" Scott recorded, "this is an awful place".

The next day they reached the Pole itself and found the camp made by Amundsen over a month before. Inside Amundsen's tent was a sheet of paper with the names of the five Norwegians who had made the historic journey. Wearily, the British party planted a Union Jack beside the Norwegian flag. Then they began the 1280-kilometre journey back to their base.

It was growing colder. Evans was terribly weak. At one point, he and Scott fell into a crevasse. Although they were hauled out, Evans never recovered from the fall.

Rations were low. Frostbite and the first stages of scurvy were affecting them all. On 16 February Evans collapsed, sick and giddy. He died early the next morning.

The others struggled on. Oates was marching in appalling pain. His toes were black and gangrene was setting in. He knew that his end was near and that he was slowing the party down. One morning he rose from his sleeping bag and muttered, "I am just going outside and may be some time." Bravely, Oates headed out into the snow to die.

The others trudged on towards the depot. On 19 March they camped down with their last two days' rations. Suddenly a blizzard started up, howling so strongly that they could not leave their tent. It raged for ten days, and the explorers knew they were finished. On 29 March, Scott wrote the last entry in his diary.

Eight months later a search party found the little green tent. Inside were the bodies of the explorers. Bowers and Wilson had died in their sleep. Scott was half out of his sleeping-bag, apparently stretching out towards Wilson.

Their tent was only seventeen kilometres from the depot and the supplies which would have saved them.

► Scott used motor sledges and Siberian ponies to haul supplies during the first stages of his second expedition. But neither proved suited to long journeys through the bitter Antarctic wastes. For the final assault, Scott and his companions hauled their sledges themselves.

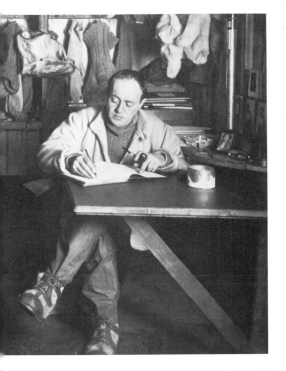

► Amundsen's Greenland huskies at the Pole. The Norwegians travelled light and killed the weakest sledge dogs for food. Amundsen spoke of his "dog cutlets" as "excellent, absolutely excellent."

▼ Captain Oates walks out into the snow to die.

The British team had scientific aims. Even during the last days they were dragging 16 kilograms of rock samples, gathered from a glacier, on their sledges.

▲ Roald Amundsen (1872-1928). In an expedition of 1903-6 he became the first man to find a North-West passage from the Atlantic, through the Arctic Sea, to the Pacific. He disappeared in 1928 while flying over the North Pole.

Gertrude Bell
A woman in Arabia

▲ Gertrude Bell's party attacked by shepherds in the Syrian desert. She kept calm, and later referred to the event as "a preposterous and provoking episode".

▲ Gertrude Bell (1868-1926) made many trips to Asia Minor and the Middle East from 1899 onwards. In 1913 she set out on her famous journey to Ha'il in the heart of Arabia.

In 1913, Gertrude Bell was making her way across the wintry Syrian desert. She was heading for Ha'il, a capital city in the heart of Arabia. Suddenly a group of wild shepherds drew near on galloping horses. Their swords flashed and rifles were fired into the air. The shepherds surrounded the party with fierce cries. One of them trained his rifle on the explorer's guides, others stripped them of their revolvers and cartridge belts.

The mood was ugly. But at that moment some of the shepherds' sheiks (leaders) rode up. By a lucky chance, they knew the guides. The danger was over and all the belongings were returned. Throughout the ordeal, the Englishwoman had kept calm.

Gertrude Bell was an extraordinary woman. The daughter of a wealthy English family, she had grown up during the prim Victorian Age. Yet she had become one of the best lady mountaineers of her day. She was a historian and archaeologist. She was an excellent linguist and spoke fluent Arabic. Above all, she was a great traveller, and was particularly drawn by the lonely magic of the desert.

In 1913, Arabia was one of the last great regions of the world which had not been fully mapped. Its people were fiercely independent and suspicious of Christian Europeans. But in December of that year, Miss Bell set out on her historic journey to Ha'il, ignoring all warnings of danger.

After the shepherds' attack, Gertrude Bell travelled on. She visited some ancient ruined forts and stopped to take measurements and copy out inscriptions.

Then she had to cross the Great Nafud, an expense of orange-red sand dunes. Here, many of the Arabs had never seen a European before. They treated the explorer well, but often demanded gifts. One sheik took Bell's revolver and binoculars.

At last the little party reached Ha'il. The mud-walled capital with its ruined battlements and lush palm groves was a true city of the wilderness. As far as Bell knew, no European had visited it for twenty years.

She was not made welcome. The ruler, Ibn Rashid, was away and the authorities would not let her travel further south as she had planned. Bell was kept almost as a prisoner.

For days she was forbidden to leave the palace and spent her time drinking tea, lounging on divans or wandering in the gardens. Was she to be killed? "It was all like a story in the Arabian Nights," she wrote. "I did not find it particularly enjoyable."

Finally, she boldly announced that she was leaving. The gamble worked. The authorities were impressed and instead of stopping her, gave all possible help for her return. She faced many more tense moments, but eventually got safely back to Damascus.

Gertrude Bell's studies of ancient sites added greatly to our knowledge of Arabian history. She had taken careful sightings of wells and water holes along her route, helping to map the desert, and she had learned much about the politics of the Arab tribes. This information proved valuable to Lawrence of Arabia in the desert campaigns of the First World War.

▲ Drawing water from a well, photographed by Gertrude Bell. The desert could be bitterly cold at night. Once, she wrote, "the men's big tent was frozen hard and they had to light fires underneath it to unfreeze the canvas".

▲ The route to Ha'il. Only one other European woman (Lady Anne Blunt) had reached the city before Gertrude Bell.

Soon after her return to Europe in 1914, the first World War began. Bell returned to the East to collect intelligence reports on Arab tribes.

41

The Challenger Deep

The descent of the *Trieste*

Sealed up inside their round steel cabin, Piccard and Walsh plunged down and down into the Pacific Ocean. The blue waters darkened as they descended, so they switched on the front floodlights. Masses of plankton (microscopic animals and plants) shimmered past. The explorers reached a depth of 720 metres. The cabin grew colder and it was pitch black outside. Piccard telephoned to the escort ships above, "We have reached the abyssal zone, the timeless world of eternal darkness."

They were now in underwater regions so deep that the sun's rays never penetrate them. And still the explorers descended. Their journey had only just begun.

It was the morning of 23 January 1960. Jacques Piccard, a Swiss scientist, and Donald Walsh, of the US Navy, were travelling down to the bed of the Challenger Deep. This lies at a depth of about 11,000 metres in an underwater region known as the Mariana Trench. It is the lowest known spot in the world.

Their craft was called the *Trieste*. It was a strange vessel with a large oblong float above and a spherical cabin below. To balance the weight of the cabin, the float was filled with petrol, which is lighter than water.

There were air tanks at each end of the float. To go down, the explorers would open the air tanks and let water in. They could also let out petrol if necessary. To rise, they would drop quantities of heavy lead shot from electrically operated containers.

Down they plunged at a rate of about one metre a second, with the pressure increasing all the time. Twice the explorers saw tiny leaks appear in their cabin. Each time they waited anxiously in case the cabin's thick steel walls should crack, letting water rush in bringing certain death. But the pressure sealed the leaks, and the *Trieste* held together.

At 8850 metres they were as far below sea level as Mount Everest is above it. Piccard began to slow down the rate of descent.

By midday they had been travelling for almost four hours and were still nowhere near the bottom. Their echo-sounders were silent, but they continued slowly in the pitch-black depths. To crash against an unsuspected underwater ridge would spell disaster.

Finally, at 10,919 metres, they touched the bottom. At this depth the water was exerting a crushing pressure of 200,000 tonnes on their craft. Outside the thick Plexiglass porthole they could see the slimy ocean bed, lit by the *Trieste*'s powerful headlights. And they noticed a flatfish gazing back at them through bulging eyes. Even at this depth and pressure life had learnt to survive and adapt.

The two men spent about 20 minutes on the ocean bed, which they claimed for science and humanity. Then they began the ascent. They broke the surface successfully after eight hours and 35 minutes underwater. They had reached the ocean's lowest depths. Now, it seemed, there was no region on earth, however remote, that humans could not lay claim to and explore.

▼ Auguste Piccard, the Swiss physicist who designed the *Trieste*, with his son Jacques.

Auguste Piccard had gained experience as a balloonist before taking up deep-sea exploration. His free-floating underwater vessels owned much to ballooning.

▼ An artist's impression of the *Trieste* on the ocean bed. It had a float filled with petrol, which is lighter than water, just as balloons contain gases which are lighter than air. The *Trieste* could rise without a connecting cable.

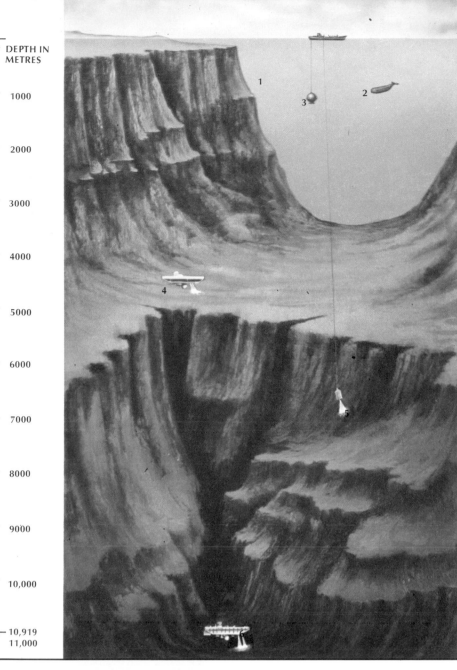

DEPTH IN
METRES

1000

2000

3000

4000

5000

6000

7000

8000

9000

10,000

10,919
11,000

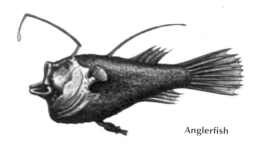

Anglerfish

▼▲ In the abyssal zone, where it is pitch-black, certain creatures have learnt to produce their own light. The anglerfish has a light on the tip of a frontal spine to lure smaller fishes into its path. Certain squids eject luminous clouds to escape their predators.

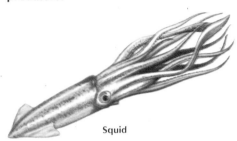

Squid

◄A diagram showing the Mariana Trench.
1 The point at which light fades out and the abyssal zone begins.
2 Whales do not dive below this point.
3 An American called William Beebe reached this depth in 1934.
4 Piccard's bathyscaphe, *FNRS 3*, reached this depth in 1954.
5 An underwater camera.
6 The *Trieste*'s dive in 1960.

▼ A diagram of Piccard's *Trieste*. He called it a *bathyscaphe* (deep-sea submersible). The float held 91,000 litres of petrol.

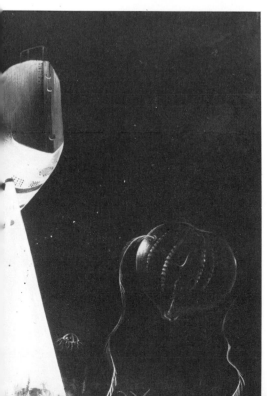

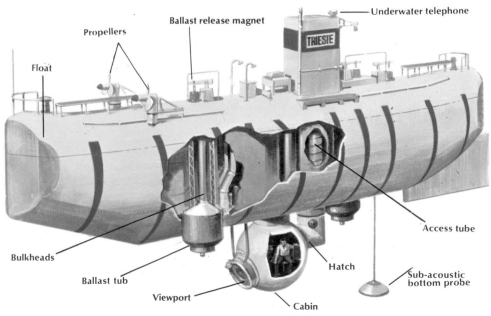

Propellers

Ballast release magnet

Underwater telephone

Float

TRIESTE

Access tube

Bulkheads

Ballast tub

Viewport

Hatch

Sub-acoustic bottom probe

Cabin

Men on the Moon
The flight of *Apollo 11*

"We have lift-off!" announced a voice at Mission Control. Slowly the huge rocket surged upwards, smoke and flame gushing from its five engines and shaking the launching pad. The date was 16 July 1969. The United States' *Saturn V* rocket was in the air. Its mission: to land the first men on the moon.

The first two stages of the rocket were soon jettisoned and the remaining craft, known as *Apollo II*, orbited the earth twice. Then Mission Control reported, "You're looking good. You're go." *Apollo II* accelerated and began its thrust towards the moon.

The moon flight took three days and was an operation of amazing complexity. Astronauts Armstrong, Aldrin and Collins had each undergone months of intensive tests and training. Every precaution had been taken to guarantee their safety, but dangers remained, especially as they came into orbit around the moon. A slight miscalculation in speed could send the craft spinning off into perpetual orbit around the sun, or propel it into a fatal collision with the surface of the moon.

But *Apollo II* entered its lunar orbit successfully. Collins remained in the command module, while Armstrong and Aldrin entered the lunar module, known as the *Eagle*. *Apollo II* divided, and the *Eagle* descended, operated by radar-guided computer.

Out of the window, Armstrong and Aldrin saw the grey surface of the Sea of Tranquillity looming closer. Armstrong took the controls and guided them towards a smooth landing spot. Back on earth, the tension was almost unbearable. Then Aldrin reported, "Tranquillity Base. The *Eagle* has landed."

The two men ate, checked their equipment and put on their moon suits. Eight and half hours after landing, Armstrong emerged from the lunar module and went down the ladder. It was 10.56 pm on 20 July. Back on earth, an estimated 1000 million viewers watched the action on television, relayed live from the moon.

▲ *Saturn V* blasts off at Cape Kennedy on 16 July, 1969.

▲ Collins orbits the moon in the command module.

▲ The *Eagle* descends, having separated from the command module.

▲ Aldrin comes down the ladder to join Armstrong on the moon's surface.

Helmet

Visor

Portable life-support system

Extra-vehicular glove

Lunar overshoe

▲ Collins never landed on the moon. His job was to orbit the moon in the command module and prepare for his companions' return. It was a lonely and nerve-racking business.

However, Armstrong and Aldrin returned successfully in the *Eagle* after 21 hours and 36 minutes on the moon's surface.

▶ Armstrong and Aldrin each wore a space suit. The portable life-support system on the back supplied oxygen, and water to cool the body (circulating through a network of tubes under the suit).

The suit was made of flexible layers of aluminium, coated nylon and Teflon. The plastic pressure helmet had a visor to protect against thermal radiation and ultraviolet/infrared light.

The astronauts collected about 20 kilograms of rock and soil samples.

Armstrong's pulse raced. "I'm at the foot of the ladder," he said. "OK. I'm going to step off the LM now. That's one small step for man, one giant leap for mankind."

He was walking on the moon. Soon, Aldrin joined him and the two men collected samples of rock and set up equipment. Then they planted the American flag on the bleak lunar surface and returned to the *Eagle*.

There was another anxious period. Would the lunar module rise, or would they be stranded? The ascent engines fired. And the *Eagle* soared up successfully towards the command module.

Armstrong and Aldrin docked with Collins and entered the command module. *Apollo II* bore them back to earth, and the eight-day mission ended with a splash-down in the Pacific Ocean.

The astronauts had returned to a planet which had already been charted by generations of explorers. But they had opened a new age of discovery; they had set foot on a world beyond our own.

▲ The command module splashes down in the Pacific.

Maps and Compasses
Reference

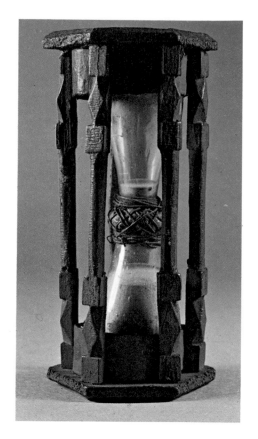

► An Italian mariner's compass of about 1580. Columbus and Magellan used compasses similar to this on their great voyages.

◄ An hourglass of the same period. It was used for keeping time at sea before the invention of high-precision clocks and chronometers.

▼ A German astrolabe of 1548, used for finding latitude.

▼ Hadley's 15-inch (38 cm) sextant of 1785.

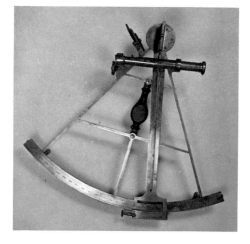

Early navigators

Long before compasses were invented, the first explorers had learnt methods of finding their way at sea.

They knew the positions of the Pole Star and other constellations in the northern sky. These gave them the position of North. Sailing south, they discovered that new stars appeared over the horizon.

They knew East from West because the sun always rises and sets in these two positions.

Cloudy days presented problems. The Vikings discovered "sunstones" (crystals of a mineral called cordierite). These refract light, so they could tell the sun's position even in dull weather.

Birds have a strange ability to find land, even when far out at sea. Watching birds migrate helped to show where land lay.

The Vikings sometimes carried ravens and released them when they were in unfamiliar waters. If the birds flew back home, they knew that the nearest land lay there. If the birds flew onwards, the Vikings knew that the nearest land lay ahead. (This method was also used by Noah.)

The compass

A splinter of lodestone (a magnetic oxide of iron) will point to the North magnetic pole when it is allowed to revolve freely.

The Ancient Chinese knew this as early as 2634 BC. But they only seem to have used their knowledge to make a kind of toy called a "south-pointing chariot". The Chinese did not make true compasses until the beginning of the 12th century AD (roughly when the compass was developed in Europe).

The first compasses were just magnetized needles fitted into straws, which were then floated in bowls of water. The straw spun till it pointed to the North.

Later, compass cards were used with pivoted needles. Sailors could then find South, East, West and all the other positions at a glance.

The compass revolutionized seafaring. In 1416, the Portuguese prince, Henry the Navigator, founded a great school of navigation to encourage exploration and improve other instruments. Many were used to find precise lines of latitude (lines which tell you how far north you are).

Latitude and longitude

Lines of latitude were found by lining an instrument up with the sun, or a familiar star, to find its exact height above the horizon. This showed how far north an explorer was.

The Arab cross-staff was one such instrument. Another was the seaman's astrolabe (developed from a similar instrument used by astronomers).

A third was the quadrant, which used a plumb line with a graded arc. This device was improved, and became the very accurate sextant early in the 18th century.

Finding longitude (how far east or west the explorer was) was much harder for 18th century seafarers. This was because they had to know the exact time at which the sun was at its highest. Sailing east, this time gets earlier than at midday in Britain. Sailing west, it gets later.

In 1714, the British Government offered a reward of £20,000 to anyone who could find a way of determining longitude at sea. This meant making a very exact clock which would keep time over long journeys despite rough seas and changes in temperature.

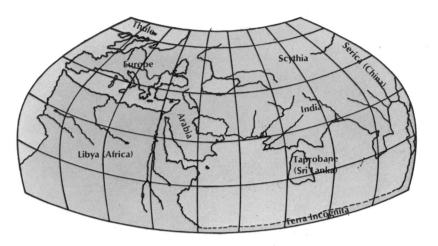

▲ Ptolemy's world map, compiled in about AD 150.

▼ The world map of Gerardus Mercator, made in 1587.

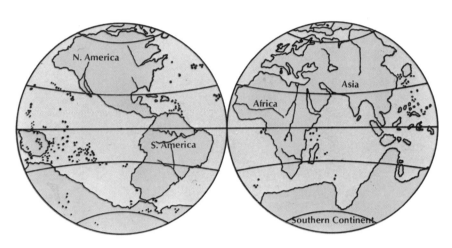

Ptolemy's map did not, of course, include America. Notice that despite the voyage of the Phoenicians, he believed that Africa stretched eastwards, enclosing the Indian Ocean and joining up with the eastern seaboard of Asia. He called the imaginary land south of the Indian Ocean *Terra Incognita* (unknown land).

Mercator's map shows new discoveries but also includes an imaginary southern continent. Belief in this vast territory continued until Captain Cook's time.

▼ The world seen from space.

Chronometers and other devices

A clockmaker called John Harrison began making highly efficient time-keepers in 1728. He developed a series of instruments leading up to his *chronometer* of 1759.

It won him £5000 of the Government's reward in 1763. But, despite improvements and countless tests, Harrison did not get all the prize money until ten years later.

Chronometers are still standard equipment on ships. However, radio communication now allows sailors to receive even more accurate time signals at sea.

There have been other changes. For thousands of years, navigators could only find the depth of water by using a plumb line or a sounding rod. This was a long business, and in the meantime the ship might be heading towards shallows or reefs.

Today sonar devices are used. They work by bouncing sound waves off the sea bed, so that its depth can be found at the flick of a switch.

Radar has also been developed, and is used to give advance warning of approaching fog or icebergs.

Early mapmakers

As explorers brought home knowledge of new lands, their information was gradually collected and pieced together to form pictures of the known world.

The first great map-makers were the Greeks. By the time of the 2nd-century geographer, Ptolemy, Europe, North Africa and Arabia had been charted with reasonable accuracy. The Greek maps included rough representations of Britain and China.

Many Greek scientists knew that the world was round. They had worked out systems of latitude and longitude. They were also experimenting with ways of showing the *round* world on *flat* parchments. This is known as "projection".

Ptolemy compiled a great world map based on a fairly accurate system of projection. Of course, he did not know about America. He was also wildly wrong about the size and shape of distant lands like India, Sri Lanka and southern Africa. Yet over 1000 years later this map was still widely used. In fact, Ptolemy estimated the circumference of the world much more accurately than Columbus did.

Developments

The great advances in mapmaking came during the age of discovery which began under Henry the Navigator.

Explorers like Columbus, Da Gama and Magellan gradually opened up the seas. In 1569 Gerardus Mercator developed a better system of projection than Ptolemy's method.

Gradually, seafarers with compasses, sextants and chronometers produced more accurate information about the places they visited. They eventually produced the world map we know today.

In our own century, the development of aviation has meant that we can photograph land and sea from the air, using planes and satellites. Aerial photography is particularly valuable for mapmakers concerned with such shifting features as cloud and ice formations, floods or widespread crop diseases. Modern weather forecasting also depends heavily on satellite photography.

However, aerial photographs have only confirmed the shape of the continents that earlier mapmakers had already revealed.

Ships
Reference

Early boats

The earliest boats were of three types: rafts, dug-out canoes, and boats with reed or wooden frameworks covered with hide, such as kayaks and coracles.

These boats were all propelled by wooden paddles. An extra-long steering oar was often added at the stern of larger boats. Sails might also be used to harness the power of the wind.

Some Stone Age peoples, like the Eskimo and Maori, have never learnt how to write or make tools of iron. However, they are very skilled sailors.

The Polynesians' expert seamanship astonished the European explorers who discovered their islands.

The Polynesians explored and colonized the islands of the Pacific, making voyages of as much as 6000 kilometres (further than Columbus travelled on his first voyage). Their favourite craft was the catamaran, a sailing boat with two hulls.

To help them navigate, they mapped the ocean swells and currents on stick charts. These were flat networks of canes. Shells were fixed to them to represent islands, and each stick stood for a current.

Keels, decks and rudders

In about 2700 BC, the Egyptians began to use planks in shipbuilding. They added a keel to strengthen the hull and give it greater stability in the water.

The Phoenicians, Greeks and Romans developed the Mediterranean war galley. This was driven by banks of oarsmen and a big, square sail. Wider merchant vessels were also built. These were mainly driven by sail and might not need oarsmen at all.

Vikings and Arabs dominated the seas during the Middle Ages. During the Crusades, Europeans began to add the Arabs' triangular lateen sails to their own craft.

Single-masted vessels gave way to two- or three-masted Crusader ships with rudders instead of oars. "Castles" were built at the prow and stern to hold fighting men. Several decks were included.

In the 15th century, the Portuguese carracks and caravels became popular. These sturdy ocean-going craft carried explorers like Columbus, Da Gama and Magellan on their great voyages of discovery.

Later developments

In the 16th and 17th centuries immense galleons were constructed for warfare. Explorers continued to use smaller ships, since large vessels were hard to steer around uncharted reefs and coastlines.

Despite the discovery of America, the riches of the East still inspired much of the maritime exploration of the period. English and Dutch adventurers were seeking a way to the East around the top of America (the North-West Passage) and Asia (the North-East Passage).

These voyages took explorers like William Barents and Henry Hudson into ice-bound Arctic seas. Here, whalers had already learnt the need for stoutly built ships.

Captain Cook used vessels similar to whaling ships on his voyages to the Arctic and Antarctic (though the *Endeavour* herself was a flat-bottomed coal ship).

No practical trade route was ever found through the bleak northern seas, but the search opened up a new age of exploration: the conquest of the polar regions.

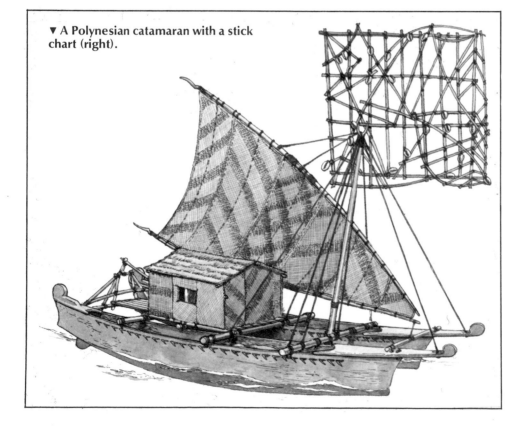

▼ A Polynesian catamaran with a stick chart (right).

▲ The naturalists' laboratory on the upper deck of *HMS Challenger*. Notice the microscopes and bottles containing samples of marine life.

◄ *HMS Challenger*, a British man-of-war, fitted out for the first global oceanographic expedition.

▲ Nansen's *Fram* caught in the drifting Arctic icepack. The "windmill" on the upper deck was used for generating electricity.

▼ A modern research ship equipped with radar, hydrophones and echo-sounding equipment.

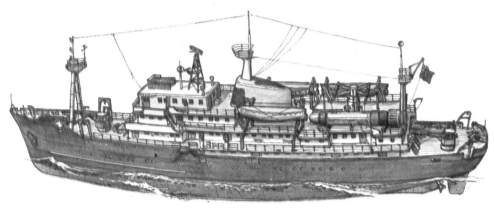

The *Fram*

The ice above the Arctic Ocean drifts constantly. In 1893, the Norwegian explorer, Fridtjof Nansen, set out to cross the North Pole in a ship frozen into the ice.

The ship was called the *Fram* and was specially built to withstand the grinding pressure of the ice.

Its boards were more than half a metre thick. The hull was saucer-shaped so that it would be lifted as much as possible above the surface as the ice pressed inwards.

In fact, the *Fram* was carried west of the Pole. Nansen and one companion failed to reach it on foot. They turned back and were eventually picked up by a British expedition.

But the *Fram* bore up superbly throughout the expedition. It finally broke free from the ice and arrived in Norway in 1896.

The *Fram* had not reached the North Pole, but Nansen had been further north than anyone before him. Later, his countryman, Roald Amundsen, borrowed the ship to reach Antarctica when he made his own historic assault on the South Pole.

The *Challenger*

By the middle of the 19th century, most of the world's coastlines were known. But scientists were only just beginning to explore the sea itself.

In 1872, *HMS Challenger* was launched on a great expedition to examine the world's oceans. She was a steam-powered wooden ship, known as a corvette, and was at sea for 3½ years. During this time, the *Challenger* sailed right round the world.

The scientists on board produced the first true charts of the ridges and trenches on the ocean floor. They dredged the seas at different levels, coming back with thousands of samples of marine life. These proved that life existed at far greater depths than had been thought possible.

Specimens were examined in chemical and naturalists' laboratories on board, and then packed into store rooms for safe keeping.

Altogether, the *Challenger* team charted 224 million square kilometres of the ocean's floor. The information they brought home filled 50 volumes of an official report. The new science of oceanography was born.

Research ships

Surface ships still carry out continuous research into the ocean depths. They carry advanced equipment such as echo-sounders, deep-sea winches and drill pipes, underwater cameras and hydrophones (underwater microphones).

Their findings tell us much about where to drill for oil, seek the best catches of fish or lay underwater cables for communications.

Hundreds of weather ships provide a constant stream of information on atmospheric conditions, which help accurate forecasting.

Research ships give us a clearer picture of the teeming life of the oceans, from the tiniest plankton to the mightiest whales.

They have also revealed much about the origins and formation of our planet.

According to many scientists, the world's continents were once joined together in a single, vast land mass. By charting the ridges and trenches of the ocean bed, we can find out how this land mass may have broken up and how the continents drifted apart.

Overland Travel

Reference

For trade, conquest and religion

Many of the first overland expeditions were made by soldiers eager for conquest. For example, Alexander the Great took his armies through Egypt, Turkestan and into India during his ten-year campaign against the Persian Empire.

Where armies have marched, priests have sometimes followed. Cortés and other conquistadors may have been brutal treasure hunters, but they also brought priests to convert new peoples, and took their missionary role very seriously.

Other missionaries made their own paths into the unknown: like Livingstone, and the French priest, Father Marquette, who explored the upper Mississippi before La Salle.

Traders such as the Polos made epic journeys to distant civilizations, and Arab merchants penetrated deep into Africa long before Europeans explored the continent.

Trade, conquest and religion inspired many expeditions long before people thought of exploring for its own sake.

Caravans

The mountains and deserts of Asia and North Africa were opened up by companies of traders and pilgrims. They travelled in large groups as protection against bandits, and their great processions were known as caravans.

Some travellers went on foot, others on horse or camel, or in covered wagons. They might camp at night under the stars, in towns, or at oases (watering places) in the desert.

If the wells were dry, disaster could follow. In 1805, an entire caravan of 2000 men and 1800 camels died between Taodemi and Timbuktu because the wells were dry.

Guides

Even compasses and sextants were of little use to travellers crossing featureless stretches of desert. Local guides were often used, and they developed great skills. Early Saharan explorers described how some guides were blind and found their way across the desert by smelling the sand.

▲ A camp in the forest, drawn from a sketch by Heinrich Barth. African explorers usually slept in tents, or in native huts.

▼ Exploring river systems held its perils. Once, on the Zambezi, Livingstone's dugout canoe was capsized by a mother hippo robbed of her young.

Sighting line

Sight

Thumb ring

▲ A camel train in Afghanistan today. Caravans still cross areas of Asia Minor and North Africa, and Tureg nomads still carry salt across remote regions of the Sahara desert.

◄ A hand-held prismatic compass. The thumb passes through the ring at the base. Landmarks are viewed through the sight at the front and aligned with the sighting line.

► H.M. Stanley in exploring kit. Notice the hat, known as a solar topee. It was used for protection against sunstroke. Sturdy knee-length boots gave protection against poisonous insects and were useful for travelling across marshy ground.

A gun was vital for shooting game, and might also be needed to ward off hostile tribes.

▼ The modern Land Rover, a versatile, all-purpose vehicle used by overland travellers today.

Interpreters

Explorers travelling among foreign peoples needed interpreters as well as guides. Cortés used a Mexican girl known as Doña Maria. She became a great favourite among the troops.

A Shoshone squaw called Sacajawea led Lewis and Clark through Indian lands when they explored the upper reaches of the Missouri from 1804 to 1806

Following rivers

The best way to penetrate uncharted country was often to follow a river. Wise explorers generally adapted to local methods of transport.

La Salle travelled by birchbark canoe. Livingstone often used native dug-outs which could be carried around swamps, falls and rapids.

When Livingstone tried to explore the Zambezi in a steamboat called the *Ma-Robert* he was beset by difficulties. Stanley had more success during his trans-African expedition of 1874 to 1877. He used a collapsible boat called the *Lady Alice*, which could be carried in five sections.

Food and equipment

Explorers on long trips had to carry bulky supplies: tools, tents, guns and ammunition, scientific instruments and medicine chests, for example.

Too much food would slow an expedition down so calculations for daily needs had to be made very carefully. Wise explorers travelled light, hoping to find fish and game along the route, and eating native foods.

Another method was to lay out food stores at depots along a route, to be picked up on the return journey. But distances and rations had to be worked out very carefully. And close understanding between expedition members was vital, as Burke and Wills found out to their cost.

A diary was an important piece of equipment. Distances, sightings, weather conditions and natural features had to be noted every day. Filling in the diary was a regular evening chore.

Even when an expedition ended tragically its achievements might live on if the diary survived.

Explorers today

There are still regions about which we know very little: the deepest forests of the Amazon, for example. But today, most exploration is carried out by scientists making studies in remote areas: archaeologists, botanists, and anthropologists.

Helicopters, inflatable rubber boats and sturdy Land Rovers now make it possible to cross even the roughest terrain.

Poles and Peaks
Reference

▼ An airship over the Arctic in about 1909. The shifting Arctic ice is best surveyed from the air.

In 1926 an American called Richard Byrd flew right over the North Pole in a seaplane. A few days later, Roald Amundsen flew over it in an airship.

▲ Robert E. Peary (1856-1920) led the first successful assault on the North Pole. He wore thick Eskimo furs and snowshoes.

The Arctic ice shifts and grinds constantly, piling up high ridges of snow or splitting apart leaving "leads" (stretches of icy water).

Once, Peary wrote, his party was "crossing a river on a succession of gigantic [ice] shingles, one, two or three feet deep and all afloat and moving".

The polar regions

The North and South Poles are the extremities of the globe. The axis of the earth, on which it revolves, runs between the Poles. (The places to which the ends of a compass needle point are called the *magnetic* poles. They are near the North and South Poles but not on the same spots).

Both areas are bitterly cold. The Arctic is a floating mass of ice, stretching from Siberia to Greenland and Alaska. It has a fairly rich wildlife of reindeer, seals, walruses and polar bears, which have supported the Eskimos for thousands of years.

The *Ant*arctic is the region around the South Pole. It is a true continent, composed of rock covered with ice and snow. But it has little wildlife except for penguins. No human foot had ever trodden on Antarctica until the first European explorers arrived in the early 19th century.

Scientific interest inspired the early exploration of the polar regions. But these bleak areas had little value for trade. The conquest of the Poles themselves was carried out in a spirit of sheer adventure.

Commander Peary

The first expedition to reach the North Pole was headed by an American naval commander called Robert Peary.

Peary made several preliminary journeys to the Arctic from 1886 onwards. In 1909 he launched his final assault, for which 50 Eskimos and 250 sledge dogs were hired.

Advance parties were sent out to set up depots along the first stretch of the route. Peary's own group of 24 men was the last to leave the base on Ellesmere Land.

The distance to the Pole was 6400 kilometres over treacherous wastes of snow and ice. When he was 200 kilometres from the Pole, Peary left the last of his parties behind and pressed on with four Eskimos and his Negro servant, Matthew Henson.

After five days of gruelling forced marches, the group reached their goal. "The Pole at last ... My dream and goal for twenty years. Mine at last! I cannot bring myself to realize it," wrote the explorer.

With Peary's success, the race for the other great prize, the South Pole, became more intense.

► A Sno-cat suspended over a crevasse during the British Commonwealth Trans-Antarctic Expedition of 1957-8.

Crevasses (deep cracks in the ice) are often hidden by layers of snow. The Sno-cats carried devices to give advance warning of crevasses, but they were not entirely reliable. If a vehicle got trapped, metal ramps were placed underneath it to help it out.

▼ Wally Herbert driving his team over an ice ridge, during his Trans-Arctic Expedition of 1968-9. You can see the ice in the foreground showing signs of melting. Herbert had to race at full stretch to avoid disaster. He reached safety on 11 June 1969.

▼ Tenzing Norgay on the summit of Mount Everest. He planted the flags of Britain, Nepal, India and the United Nations on the peak.

Notice the oxygen mask. Though Tenzing was a hardy Sherpa from the Himalayas, even he found breathing a problem at this height.

Both he and Hillary had to carry masses of equipment: ropes, ladders, ice-picks and supplies. But their path to the summit had been prepared by advance parties carrying loads and cutting steps in the ice so that they could save their energy for the final assault.

Further exploration

Polar exploration continued long after the conquests of the North and South Poles.

In 1912–13, an Australian expedition headed by Douglas Mawson surveyed 160 kilometres of the Antarctic coastline. Two members died during the expedition.

In 1915, Ernest Shackleton planned to cross Antarctica from coast to coast. His expedition failed disastrously, and his goal was not achieved until 1958, when Vivian Fuchs led the British Commonwealth Trans-Antarctic Expedition.

Fuchs's expedition used Sno-cats (tracked vehicles specially designed for polar exploration). But despite such advances in equipment and machinery, the older method of dog-sledging still appeals to many polar travellers.

Between 1968 and 1969, an Englishman called Wally Herbert crossed the Arctic on foot with three companions. They reached the North Pole on 6 April 1969, then raced against time to reach Spitzbergen before the ice melted in the summer sunshine.

Mountaineering

Mountaineers face problems similar to those of polar explorers: snow and ice, the danger of frostbite, snow-blindness and constant hardship.

A few enthusiasts had climbed mountains before De Saussure's expedition. But after it the sport of mountaineering became a widespread craze.

Ropes, ice-picks and crampons (metal spikes on the sole of the boot) were used. One after another, the peaks of the Alps were scaled. In 1865, the challenging Matterhorn was conquered, but during the descent a rope broke and four men died.

After the Alps, mountaineers began to look for new challenges: the peaks of Africa, America and Asia. And, in 1953, a British expedition led by Edmund Hillary and Tenzing Norgay finally conquered the highest peak in the world, Mount Everest, which stands 8850 metres above sea level.

The air is thin at this height. Both Tenzing and Hillary wore oxygen masks. In 1978, their feat was repeated by a team who made the ascent without breathing equipment.

Underwater Exploration
Reference

Diving bells and submarines

According to legend, Alexander the Great was once lowered to the sea bed in a glass barrel in order to observe marine life. It seems unlikely. A method of piping pressurized air down to a diving bell was only invented in 1690, by Edmund Halley.

Diving bells could only be winched up or down from a surface craft. In 1776 an American called David Bushnell invented the first steerable submarine. It was called the *Turtle* and was driven by one man operating propellers.

During the American Civil War of 1861–5, a submarine called the *Hunley* was used for the first time to sink an enemy vessel. The submarine's value in warfare soon became clear.

Powered submarines were developed throughout the 19th century. In 1907 the Germans produced their highly efficient U-boats which caused havoc in the First World War.

After the Second World War, nuclear power was harnessed. On 3 August 1953, an American nuclear submarine called *Nautilus* passed right under the North Pole.

The lower depths

Submarines are not suitable for exploring at great depths because of the pressure of the water on the hull.

An American called William Beebe designed a vessel specially for this purpose. It was known as a *bathysphere* (depth sphere) and was made of thick steel.

Beebe's bathysphere could carry two people. It had its own oxygen supply and was winched up and down by a cable attached to its escort ship. In 1934, Beebe made a dive of 908 metres in his bathysphere.

Then, in 1948, Auguste Piccard began to develop his revolutionary bathyscaphes. Their advantage was that they could go up and down freely without the need for a connecting cable. Piccard's first craft was called *FNR3*, and his next was the *Trieste*.

Nine years after the historic descent of the *Trieste*, Piccard's son Jacques launched an expedition to explore the warm Gulf Stream in a new kind of craft. It was called the *Ben Franklin* and was specially designed to travel in the middle depths of the ocean.

▲ Halley's diving bell. It was weighted down with blocks of lead. Air was piped into it from a barrel outside the vessel. A second diver with a helmet could walk around outside on the sea bed.

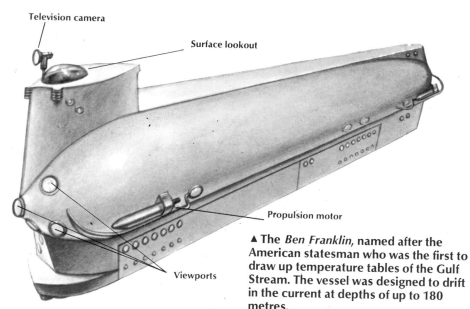

Television camera

Surface lookout

Propulsion motor

Viewports

▲ The *Ben Franklin*, named after the American statesman who was the first to draw up temperature tables of the Gulf Stream. The vessel was designed to drift in the current at depths of up to 180 metres.

▼ The United States' nuclear submarine *Nautilus*. On 3 August 1958, she passed beneath the North Pole, guided by her commander, William Anderson. In some places, the ice above her was 19 metres thick.

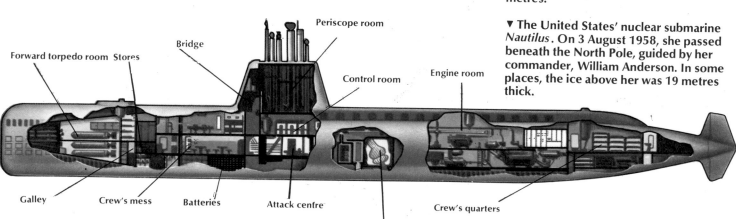

Periscope room

Bridge

Forward torpedo room Stores

Control room

Engine room

Galley

Crew's mess

Batteries

Attack centre

Reactor

Crew's quarters

Diving suits

Halley's diving bell included an attachment for divers to walk around the craft, using pressurized air piped from the bell.

At these lower depths water exerts a crushing pressure on the lungs, so specially reinforced diving suits were needed. The first completely closed suit, with a heavy metal helmet, was invented by Augustus Siebe in 1837. At great depths, closed suits are still used.

The aqualung

Siebe's divers still needed a connecting pipe through which to receive air. Divers were freed from this in 1943, when Jacques Cousteau invented the first "aqualung". This consisted of compressed air cylinders, a mouthpiece and a "demand regulator" which fed the diver exactly the amount of compressed air needed.

Even more revolutionary developments are now taking place. Recently, scientists have been experimenting with portable plastic "gills" which extract oxygen from the water exactly as those of fishes do.

Living underwater

Two-thirds of the world's surface is covered by the sea. We need to make full use of its food and mineral resources.

Cousteau pioneered the development of underwater laboratories where "aquanauts" could live for days on end.

The first was called *Conshelf I*, and was set up in 1962. Later, Cousteau designed two more underwater *habitats* (living areas). In *Conshelf III*, six aquanauts spent three weeks at a depth of 100 metres.

The United States developed similar *Sealab* projects. In the *Sealab III* experiment of 1969, five 8-man teams took turns to live for 12 days each at a depth of 183 metres.

In these habitats, scientists have examined the possibility of farming the sea bed. They have also learnt much about the effects of underwater living on the aquanauts themselves.

Dangers

Early compressed-air systems used mixtures of oxygen and nitrogen. But nitrogen can cause a giddy drunkenness known to divers as the "rapture of the deep". If a diver rises too quickly to the surface, the nitrogen present in the bloodstream may bubble up, causing a disease known as "the bends". This can result in death.

Today, compressed air is usually a mixture of oxygen and helium, a gas which is lighter and much safer than nitrogen.

▲ A diver of 1905 faces peril from an octopus. The heavy helmet, chest-piece and air pipe restricted the movement of early divers.

▲ The aqualung freed divers, allowing them to explore sunken wrecks and observe marine life. Here, a diver is shown bringing up a Greek vase.

▲ *Tektite II*, an American underwater habitat. Here, in 1970, several aquanauts lived and conducted experiments for two-week periods.

Their underwater home was 15 metres beneath the Caribbean Sea. Scientists observed their behaviour to see how they stood up to stressful conditions.

Exploring Space
Reference

Telescopes

Early astronomers made their observations with the naked eye. Ptolemy believed that the earth was the centre of the universe, and that the sun, moon and planets revolved around it.

Ptolemy's belief was widely held. Then, in about 1600, the first telescope was made by a Dutch spectacle-maker. It allowed astronomers to explore the heavens in more detail.

Galileo (1564–1642) discovered that there were mountains and craters on the moon. He also proved that the earth and planets revolve around the sun, as Copernicus and some other astronomers had already suggested.

Later, Sir Isaac Newton (1642–1727) invented a reflecting telescope which gave greater magnification and detail than Galileo's had.

We still use reflecting telescopes. America's immense reflector on Mount Palomar has a mirror more than 5 metres wide. Russia has an even bigger telescope, with a 6-metre mirror.

Scientists have also developed radio telescopes. These pick up radio waves coming from deep in space.

The space race

The earth has a strong gravitational pull. To escape it, a spacecraft must reach a speed of more than 11.13 kilometres *per second*. Speeds of this sort only became possible with the development of rocket power.

The first rocket powered by liquid fuel was launched in the United States in 1926. During the Second World War the Germans developed their deadly V-2 rockets, which carried explosive warheads.

Then, in 1957, the Russians put a rocket into space to launch their first satellite, *Sputnik I*.

The following year, the Americans replied with a satellite of their own, and soon a space race began.

In April 1961 the Russian astronaut Yuri Gagarin became the first man in space. America sent up Colonel John Glenn the following year.

In March 1965 the Russians achieved the first space walk. Alexei Leonov left his *Voskhod* spacecraft and drifted in space, attached to his craft by a safety line.

The Americans then overtook the Russians by achieving the first space docking between two craft. And in 1969 they landed men on the moon.

▲ The nearside of the moon.

◄ Russian cosmonauts Yuri Gagarin and Valentina Tereshkova. Tereshkova became the first woman in space during a 71-hour flight in 1963.

▼ America's vast reflecting telescope at Mount Palomar is set in heavy mountings to avoid vibration. Compare its size to that of the human figure.

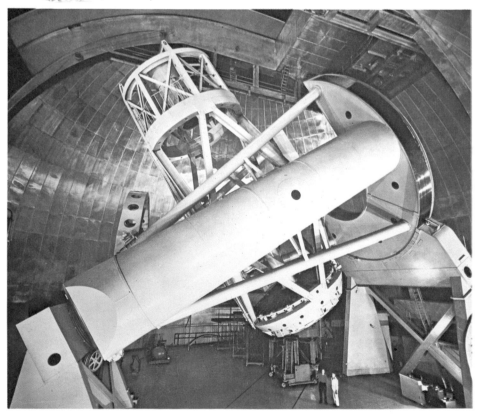

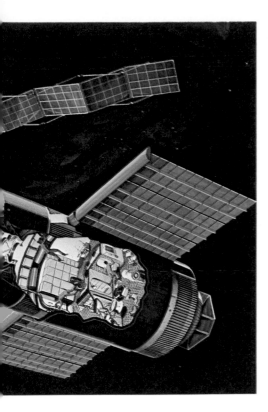

◄ *Skylab*, the space observatory which fell to earth in 1979.

▼ An artist's impression showing how the orbiting space shuttle will be launched by its booster rockets.

Further exploration

Further exploration of the moon continued after the historic landing of 1969. The Russians placed a self-propelled vehicle on the moon in 1970. The following year, *Apollo 15* astronauts Scott and Irwin explored the moon's surface in their Lunar Roving Vehicle.

Unmanned probes have also been directed at Venus, Mars, Mercury and other planets. But no one has yet landed on any of the planets. The space race has become far less intense than it was in the 1960s.

Space stations

The 1970s saw the development of the great space stations: the Russian *Salyut* and the American *Skylab*. These orbiting laboratories circled the earth in space, manned by crews who remained there for weeks on end.

One purpose was to study the universe in greater detail than astronomers can on earth. In space, faint radiation from distant galaxies can be received more easily than on earth, whose atmosphere is too thick for them to penetrate. From *Salyut* and *Skylab*, astronauts were also able to make detailed surveys of weather conditions on earth.

Above all, the space stations gave scientists a chance to see how astronauts could stand up to long periods of weightlessness. The effects on the mind and body were studied in detail. Experiments were conducted to find out whether seeds could be grown in the artifical atmosphere of the space stations. Tests of this sort are vital if we are to colonize worlds beyond our own.

The life of the space stations is limited. In 1979, *Skylab* began to break up. It was brought down to earth in an atmosphere of great drama, because scientists could not be sure exactly where it would crash. In fact, it fell to earth without killing anyone, far from habitation in the deserts of Australia.

The space shuttle

Launching rockets for space travel is a massively expensive business, since each craft can only be used once. Many stages will be jettisoned before it returns to earth.

In 1980, America plans to launch its new space-shuttle project. A winged spacecraft, looking like a plane, will be launched by booster rockets. It will carry a heavy payload of materials for building space stations.

Once in space, the craft will be able to orbit and return to earth intact, where it will re-load and take off again. In this way it will operate as a "shuttle" between earth and space.

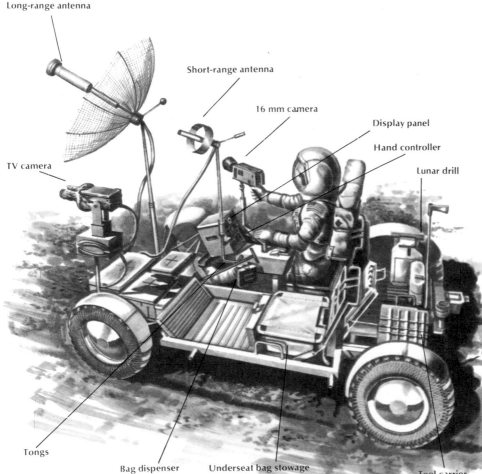

Long-range antenna

Short-range antenna

16 mm camera

Display panel

Hand controller

Lunar drill

TV camera

Tongs

Bag dispenser

Underseat bag stowage

Tool carrier

▲ The Lunar Roving Vehicle used by *Apollo 15* astronauts Scott and Irwin. It could travel at 16 kph.

The vehicle was electrically powered, and steered by a T-bar control column between the seats.

Ready Reference

Glossary

Antarctic: the regions around the South Pole, roughly within the Antarctic Circle: latitude 66° 33′ S.

Aqualung: a portable breathing apparatus for divers. Compressed air cylinders are strapped to the back and feed air to a face-mask.

Arctic: the regions around the North Pole, roughly within the Arctic Circle: latitude 66° 33′ N.

Astrolabe: an instrument for measuring the height of a star above the horizon. Used to find a position at sea.

Avalanche: a rapid fall of rock, snow or ice on a mountain.

Aztecs: a Mexican people whose civilization began to flourish around Lake Texcoco in AD 1345.

Bathyscaphe: a deep-sea submersible, of the free-floating type invented by Auguste Piccard.

Bathysphere: a sphere for deep-sea exploration, attached to a cable and winch. The type was invented by William Beebe.

Bends (the): caisson disease, which may be caused when a diver rises too quickly from the ocean depths. Nitrogen present in the bloodstream bubbles up, sometimes with fatal results.

Brigantine: a two-masted sailing ship of the 16th to 19th centuries.

Caravan: a party of several merchants or pilgrims travelling together in the desert.

Caravel: a small, speedy sailing ship of the type used by Portuguese and Spanish explorers in the 15th to 17th centuries.

Cathay: the name under which northern China was known in Marco Polo's time.

Chronometer: a very precise time-keeper used in navigation. Its accuracy is not affected by changes in temperature or rough seas.

Compass: a direction-finding instrument showing the position of the magnetic North Pole, and so indicating all other positions.

Conquistadors (conquerors): the 16th century Spanish invaders who subdued Central and South America.

Crampon: a metal spike, or arrangement of spikes on the sole of a boot, used in mountaineering to give a good grip on ice.

Crevasse: a deep crack in the ice.

Cross-staff: an instrument for measuring the height of a star above the horizon. Used to find a position at sea.

Delta: the area at the mouth of a river where its different branches run into the sea.

Dhow: lateen-rigged Arab ship.

Diving bell: an open-bottomed vessel used for exploring the sea bed.

Equator: an imaginary line circling the earth at a point equally distant from both the North and South Poles.

Frostbite: inflammation or decomposition of a part of the body due to extreme cold.

Galley: a long, square-sailed ship of the ancient world, often propelled by banks of oarsmen.

Glacier: a frozen river of ice moving slowly down a mountainside.

Habitat: an underwater living area, such as *Sealab* or *Conshelf*.

Hydrophone: an underwater microphone.

Lateen sail: a triangular sail used on Arab dhows and later adopted by European shipbuilders.

Latitude (line of): an imaginary line showing a map position in degrees north or south of the equator.

Lead: a split which opens up in polar ice and reveals the water below.

Litter: a vehicle containing a couch, carried on the shoulders of people or by pack animals.

Longitude (line of): an imaginary line showing a map position in degrees east or west of a fixed point (usually Greenwich, England)

Muslim: a believer in the Islamic religion founded by the prophet Mohammed (also known as a Mohammedan, or, during the Crusades, a Saracen).

North-East Passage: a route to the East which European explorers searched for by trying to sail around the north coast of Asia.

North-West Passage: a route to the East which European explorers searched for by trying to sail around the north coast of America.

Pancake ice: floating discs of newly-formed ice at sea.

Pillars of Hercules: the ancient name for the Straits of Gibraltar.

Poles (North and South): the northern and southern extremities of the earth, between which the earth revolves on its axis.

Poles (North and South magnetic): places near the North and South Poles towards which the ends of a compass needle point.

Pole Star: a bright star in the constellation of the Little Bear. It appears almost directly above the North Pole.

Radar: a method of detecting an object such as a ship; or a coastline, by bouncing radio waves off it.

Radio telescope: a telescope designed to receive radio waves from deep in space.

Reflecting telescope: a telescope in which the image received is reflected by a mirror or mirrors to give a clearer image.

Scurvy: a disease which used to afflict sailors on long voyages. It was caused by the lack of vitamin C in their diet. (This vitamin is found in fresh fruit and vegetables.)

Serica: the name by which China was known to the ancients.

Sextant: an instrument with a graded arc used for surveying and position-finding both on land and sea. It was developed from the earlier quadrant.

Sheik: an Arab chief, or the headman of an Arab village.

Sno-cat: a tracked vehicle designed for polar exploration.

Snow blindness: blindness caused by the dazzling reflection of sunlight on snow; a hazard for both polar explorers and mountaineers.

Snowshoe: a broad, racket-shaped piece of footwear which spreads the body's weight and so allows the wearer to cross snow-fields without sinking.

Solar topee: a type of hat often worn by explorers in hot climates to give protection against sunstroke.

Sonar: echo-sounding equipment used to detect objects by bouncing sound waves off them.

Strait: a narrow seaway separating two large land masses.

Terra Australis (the Southern Land): the imaginary continent which early mapmakers believed lay in the southern half of the globe.

Thule: an island north of Britain referred to by Pytheas. Its true location is not known.

Timbuktu: an ancient Muslim trading and religious centre south of the Sahara. Legends of mystery and romance surrounded it until the first Europeans returned with eye-witness descriptions in the middle of the 19th century.

Tin Isles: the Greek name for the British Isles.

▲ Triumph and tragedy: Captain Scott's doomed party at the South Pole. Their faces show their disappointment. They had just learnt that Roald Amundsen's Norwegian team had reached the Pole before them.

Further reading

Conquistadores: Meridel LeSueur (Franklin Watts, 1973)
Cooper's Creek: Alan Moorehead (St. Martin's Press, 1976)
Discovery Under the Southern Cross: Roselyn Poignant (Franklin Watts, 1976)
Exploration and Discoveries: Irving Robbin (Grosset and Dunlap)
Explorers: Richard Humble (Time-Life, 1978)
Explorers into Africa: Josephine Kamm (Macmillian, 1970)
Exploring Space: Roy Worvill (Merry Thoughts)
Explorers of the Arctic and Antarctic: Edward F. Dolan Jr. (Macmillan, 1968)
Exploring Under the Sea: Brian Williams (Franklin Watts, 1979)
Famous Discoverers and Explorers of America: Charles H. Johnston (Arno Books, reprint of 1917 edition)
Famous Firsts in Exploration: Herbert M. Mason Jr. (G.P. Putnam's Sons, 1967)
First Book of New World Explorers: Louise D. Rich (Franklin Watts, 1960)
First over the Oceans: Melinda Blau (Silver Burdett, 1978)

First to the Moon: Jim Collins (Silver Burdett, 1978)
First to the Top of the World: Tom Lisker (Silver Burdett, 1978)
A History of African Exploration: David Mountfield (Sky Harbor Books, 1976)
A History of Polar Exploration: David Mountfield (Dial Press, 1974)
Journeys Down the Amazon: J.M. Cohen (Transatlantic Books, 1976)
They Put out to Sea: The Story of the Map: Roger Duvoisin (Alfred A. Knopf, 1944)
Voyages of Discovery: J.M. Claessen (British Book Center, 1977)

Biographies
Captain Cook and the South Pacific: Oliver Warner and J.C. Beaglehole (American Heritage, 1963)
Captain Scott: L. Dugarde Peach (Merry Thoughts)
Columbus and the Discovery of America: John Langdon-Davies (Viking Press, 1972)
Heroes of Polar Exploration: Ralph K. Andrist and George J. Dufek (American Heritage, 1962)
The Life of Captain James Cook: J.C. Beaglehole (Stanford University Press, 1974)
Livingstone: Tim Jeal (Dell, 1974)
Magellan: First Around the World: Ronald Syme (William Morrow, 1953)

Marco Polo: Richard Humble (G.P. Putnam's Sons, 1975)
Scott of the Antarctic: Elspeth Huxley (Atheneum Press, 1978)

First-hand accounts
The Vinland Sagas and the Norse Discovery of the New World: translated by Magnus Magnusson and Hermann Palsson (Penguine Books, 1965)
The Travels of Marco Polo: translated by Ronald Latham (Penguin Books, 1958)
Four Voyages to the New World: translated by R.H. Major (Peter Smith)
The Conquest of New Spain: translated by John M. Cohen (Penguin Books, 1963)

Index